George C. Marshall

SOLDIER OF PEACE

"Our policy is directed not against any country

or doctrine but against hunger, poverty, desperation and chaos.

Its purpose should be the revival of a working economy

in the world so as to permit the emergence of

political and social conditions in which

free institutions can exist."

Secretary of State George C. Marshall articulating
the general principles of the Marshall Plan in an address
at Harvard University on June 5, 1947

George C. Marshall

SOLDIER OF PEACE

With an essay by Larry I. Bland

A Personal Reflection on
George C. Marshall

by Colin L. Powell

Catalogue by James G. Barber

THE NATIONAL PORTRAIT GALLERY

SMITHSONIAN INSTITUTION

AND

THE GEORGE C. MARSHALL FOUNDATION

1997

An exhibition at the
NATIONAL PORTRAIT GALLERY
Washington, D.C.
November 7, 1997–July 12, 1998

THE GEORGE C. MARSHALL FOUNDATION
Lexington, Virginia
August 28, 1998–February 28, 1999

This catalogue and the exhibition have been made possible
by a generous grant from the Bayer Corporation Pharmaceutical Division.

Distributed by The Johns Hopkins University Press

ISBN: 0-8018-5814-3

LIBRARY OF CONGRESS CATALOGING-IN-PUBLICATION DATA

Barber, James. 1952–
    George C. Marshall, soldier of peace / with an essay by Larry I. Bland :
catalogue by James G. Barber.
        p.   cm.
    "A personal reflection on George C. Marshall by Colin L. Powell."
    Published in association with Johns Hopkins University Press.
    "An exhibition at the National Portrait Gallery, Washington, D.C.,
November 7, 1997–July 12, 1998 [and] The George C. Marshall Foundation,
Lexington, Virginia, August 28, 1998–February 28, 1999"— T.p. verso.
    Includes bibliographical references (p.   ) and index.
    ISBN 0-8018-5814-3
    1. Marshall. George C. (George Catlett), 1880-1959—Portraits—
Exhibitions. 2. Statesmen—United States—Portraits—Exhibitions.
I. Bland, Larry I. II. Powell, Colin L. III. National Portrait Gallery
(Smithsonian Institution) IV. George C. Marshall Foundation. V. Title.
E745.M37B37   1997
973.918'092—dc21
[B]   97-34989
                                                                 CIP

COVER:
George C. Marshall by Ernest Hamlin Baker (1889–1975).
Watercolor on board, 27.3 x 23.5 cm. (10¾ x 9¼ in.), 1947
The George C. Marshall Foundation

FRONTISPIECE:
George C. Marshall by Thomas Edgar Stephens (1886–1966).
Oil on canvas, 127 x 101.6 cm. (50 x 40 in.), circa 1949.
National Portrait Gallery, Smithsonian Institution;
transfer from the National Gallery of Art;
gift of Ailsa Mellon Bruce, 1951

Contents

Chronology

1880
December 31: Born in Uniontown, Pennsylvania

1897–1901
Is a cadet at Virginia Military Institute, Lexington, Virginia

1902
February 2: Commissioned second lieutenant of infantry, United States Army

February 11: Marries Elizabeth C. Coles of Lexington, Virginia

1902–1903
Serves with the Thirtieth Infantry Regiment, Philippine Islands

1903–1906
Serves at Fort Reno, Oklahoma

1906
Detailed as a student at the Infantry and Cavalry School, Fort Leavenworth, Kansas

1907
March: Promoted to first lieutenant

1908–1910
Serves as an instructor, Fort Leavenworth, Kansas

1916
July: Promoted to captain

1917–1918
Serves with American Expeditionary Forces, France

1919
May: Appointed aide-de-camp to General John J. Pershing

1920
July: Promoted to major

1923
August: Promoted to lieutenant colonel

1924–1927
Serves with the Fifteenth Infantry Regiment, Tientsin, China

1927
September 15: Death of Elizabeth Coles Marshall

October: Appointed assistant commandant, Infantry School, Fort Benning, Georgia

1930
October 15: Marries Katherine Tupper Brown

1933
June: Appointed commandant, Fort Moultrie, South Carolina, and to Civilian Conservation Corps District I

September: Promoted to colonel

1936
October: Promoted to brigadier general

1936–1938
Serves as commandant of the Fifth Brigade, Third Division, Vancouver Barracks, Washington

1938
July: Appointed assistant chief of staff, War Plans Division, War Department, Washington, D.C.

October: Appointed deputy chief of staff

1939
September 1: Sworn in as chief of staff

1941–1945
Oversees recruiting, training, equipping, and deploying of United States Army during World War II

1945
November: Resigns as chief of staff

December–January 1947: Serves as President Harry Truman's special representative to China

1947
January: Appointed secretary of state

June 5: Proposes aid to Europe (Marshall Plan) in speech at Harvard

1948
January 5: Is *Time* magazine's Man of the Year for 1947

1949
January: Resigns as secretary of state

October: Becomes president of the American Red Cross

1950
September: Serves as secretary of defense until September 1951

1953
December: Awarded Nobel Peace Prize

1959
October 16: Dies at Walter Reed Army Hospital, Washington, D.C.

October 20: Buried at Arlington National Cemetery

Foreword

It is fitting that the National Portrait Gallery should join the George C. Marshall Foundation to celebrate the career of a remarkable American. George Catlett Marshall was exceptional in many respects. A military man by training and profession, his greatest legacy is the European Recovery Program—the "Marshall Plan"—which enabled the Western European nations to rebuild in peace after the devastation of the Second World War. He was (in Drew Middleton's words) a "plainspoken, untheatrical character in an era that abounded with . . . military and political prima donnas." A visionary without the usual trappings, neither a brilliant writer nor spellbinding orator, Marshall nonetheless communicated powerfully, creating a sense of unquestioned credibility.

Marshall served with distinction in the First World War, but his career bloomed slowly during the interwar period. His qualities of leadership came to the fore as war in Europe once again approached, and Franklin Roosevelt named him chief of staff of the army on September 1, 1939, the day on which Hitler's forces invaded Poland. General Marshall served as chief of staff throughout World War II, and after hostilities ended, he was asked by President Harry S. Truman to assist him in foreign policy matters that urgently needed attention.

Few military leaders in history can have so clearly confronted the realities of global politics as did Marshall in the postwar years. Sent by President Truman to China in late 1945, with the rank of ambassador, he tried unsuccessfully to negotiate a peace between Mao Tse-tung's rising Communist Party and Chiang Kai-shek's Nationalists. In configuring his plan for European postwar recovery in 1947, he provided a framework for both the rebuilding of the war-ravaged combatant states and the "Cold War" division between the Soviet-dominated East and the increasingly Americanized West. As secretary of defense, shortly after the beginning of the Korean War, Marshall again faced the problem of American confrontation with China—a bitter policy conflict that culminated in the dismissal of General Douglas MacArthur when he threatened to use maximum force against Mao's China.

Although these problems were resolved ambiguously, and none to the full satisfaction of the American side, Marshall's reputation for intelligence, integrity, and discipline emerged unscathed. His receipt of the Nobel Peace Prize in 1953 attested to the regard in which he was held internationally.

In this book, and in its accompanying exhibition, historian James Barber has brought together documents that combine to make an eloquent portrait of this notable leader. It is particularly appropriate that this should take place on the fiftieth anniversary of the Marshall Plan, and at a time when world attention is once again focused on both economic and military alliances in Europe. In the post–Cold War era, the challenges are very different from what Truman and Marshall faced fifty years ago. A number of smaller nations have emerged, amidst stubborn ethnic and territorial conflicts. The larger nations have formed a European Community, but the road to new trade and currency arrangements has not been smooth. NATO, the military alliance configured after World War II to maintain stability, must now consider how to deal with neighboring countries that had formerly been hostile but now wish to participate in cooperative peacekeeping efforts.

Thus, the lessons of the Marshall era are worth studying once again. We appreciate the generosity of the lenders to our exhibition, the splendid support of the Bayer Corporation Pharmaceutical Division, and the contributions of the distinguished authors who have participated so graciously in this book.

ALAN FERN
Director, National Portrait Gallery

ALBERT J. BEVERIDGE III
President, George C. Marshall Foundation

George C. Marshall

LARRY I. BLAND

People in public life tend to fall into two groups, Secretary of War Henry L. Stimson once said: those who thought primarily of what they could do for the job that they held, and those who thought of what the job could do for them. He put George Catlett Marshall, the first American military leader to be a truly global commander, at the top of his list in the first category. "You are one of the most selfless public officials that I have ever known," he said on December 31, 1942, Marshall's sixty-second birthday.[1] The man Stimson praised was an austere, demanding, efficient leader, whose cool blue eyes seemed to penetrate to the core of interlocutors; yet he had a saving sense of humor and a passion for simple justice.[2]

George Marshall's family and its circumstances had considerable impact upon the development of those values and behavior that people admire most in him. He was reared in a quintessentially American small town—Uniontown, Pennsylvania, southeast of Pittsburgh and a dozen miles north of the Mason-Dixon Line. Born on the last day of 1880, he was reared in Victorian middle-class respectability in the last house on the western edge of town. His parents had Virginia and Kentucky roots; Marshall's siblings—brother Stuart, nearly six years older, and sister Marie, five years older—were born in

Kentucky. Young George was the only one born in the North, and he retained throughout his life portions of his western Pennsylvania accent. His father, George Sr., was a successful manufacturer of coke for blast furnaces. But in 1890 and 1891, he invested heavily in the land boom in Virginia, losing most of his modest fortune when the bubble burst; the family was reduced to genteel poverty that required a decade to overcome. Marshall admired his father's honesty and diligence in repaying his creditors.

Marshall's father was intellectually curious, a tinkerer constantly experimenting with new ways of doing things and improving his family's life. Clearly he communicated these values to his youngest son. He also inculcated in George a love of the outdoors, particularly of hunting and fishing. But probably most important, Marshall's father was interested in history, particularly the history that had flowed by on the National Road before the family's front door. The sites of George Washington's Fort Necessity (1754) and General Edward Braddock's defeat and grave (1755) were just east of Uniontown. He often took his son to visit these and other historically significant places.

As a child, George was somewhat casually educated in private Uniontown schools, but after 1891 he matriculated at the local public school, when the family's finances required it. Much to his father's dismay, he demonstrated little aptitude except in history. Marshall retained his interest in history throughout his life. As Richard Neustadt and Ernest May have observed in *Thinking in Time*, Marshall somehow developed the habit of "seeing time as a stream": applying a con-

General George C. Marshall arriving at the Capitol, December 1945, to testify before a joint committee of Congress, which is investigating military preparedness during the Japanese attack on Pearl Harbor.

The George C. Marshall Foundation

sciousness of past problems, ideas, and solutions to the present rather than seeing every current problem in isolation and thus as new and unique.[3]

In 1897 young Marshall insisted that he wished to attend the Virginia Military Institute, like his older brother, who had graduated in 1894 and was an industrial chemist. The cost was considerable, and Stuart was skeptical that George could handle the rigorous physical, military, and academic schedule. Stuart's opposition made George all the more determined, and his mother sold some property to raise the tuition.[4]

At the Virginia Military Institute, Marshall blossomed. Initially he was an outsider, one of a handful of northerners at this intensely southern school and the only one in the class of 1901 to stay all four years. Robert E. Lee and Stonewall Jackson were both buried in Lexington, where VMI is located, and Jackson had taught at VMI before going off to war in 1861. Marshall once observed that he had been "greatly influenced by the traditions concerning General Lee and General Jackson."[5]

Academically Marshall began and ended his four years at VMI unexceptionally, but read "pretty much anything I could get my hands on." But in the military aspects of VMI life, he was outstanding, holding the highest available cadet rank during his last three years. The rigors of life there he accepted more stoically than most cadets: "It was part of the business and the only thing to do was to accept it as best you could and as easily as you could."[6] Indeed, throughout his life he worked within whatever system confronted him, seeking to reform rather than to overthrow it.

Marshall was "very exacting and exact" in his military duties. He had significant responsibilities, and he had learned to discipline himself. His success at VMI had demonstrated to him that his ambitions for a military career could be fulfilled. Marshall was, VMI's superintendent wrote in a 1901 letter of recommendation to President William McKinley, "fully the equal of the best" West Point graduates.[7]

Fortunately for Marshall, the United States Army was expanding in the wake of the Spanish-American War and the Philippine insurrection. In the autumn of 1901, he passed a written examination for officer candidates and was offered a commission in the infantry (last in the rough order of branch status at the time). In February 1902, commission in hand, he could afford to marry his VMI sweetheart, Lexington beauty Elizabeth ("Lily") Carter Coles. The couple had a short honeymoon in Washington, D.C., before Marshall had to depart for his first posting on the island of Mindoro in the Philippines. The wives of second lieutenants were not permitted to go, and Lily's always-delicate health was also an obstacle.

The army did not provide lieutenants with leadership training in those days, but on the transport from San Francisco to Manila, new officers who had served with the volunteers during the recent war "were very industrious in telling me, particularly, who had come from civil life, how I should function. They understood it all. Later on I discovered they knew damn little."[8]

Marshall was only in the Philippines for eighteen months, from May 1902 to November 1903, but he used his time wisely. The isolation his small command faced in southern Mindoro made him virtually the governor of that area, allowing him to practice his new profession without constant oversight by higher authority. Later, when he was transferred to Santa Mesa, near Manila, and was confined to quarters with a broken ankle, he used the time helping the local inspector general clear up the paperwork of the demobilizing army. "I became quite an expert on papers," he later recalled. "It helped me a great deal in later years."[9]

He returned to the United States at the end of 1903 and spent the next thirty-two months at Fort Reno, Oklahoma, a typical old army post created to control the Indians. There was plenty of time for recreation, and occasionally he would receive an interesting assignment—such as mapping an area of the Texas-Mexico border around Langtry and Del Rio. But when the chance presented itself, he asked for an assignment to the Infantry and Cavalry School at Fort Leavenworth.

Many officers at the time were skeptical of, or hostile to, the school, but Marshall recognized that its new curriculum was on the cutting edge. Marshall, still a second lieutenant, was the lowest-ranking student. He was also shocked to discover that most of the other students were better prepared than he, and he was not thought to be one of the prime candidates for the crucial second-year advanced course. Marshall reacted as he had upon hearing his older brother's disparagement of his chances at VMI: he would show them. "I knew I would have to study harder than I ever dreamed of studying before in my life."[10]

George C. Marshall, seated third from left, with the VMI cadet staff, 1900-1901. *The George C. Marshall Foundation*

In class, Marshall was immediately impressed with, and inspired by, one of the new instructors, Major John F. Morrison. Others taught regulations and technique, Marshall thought; Morrison "spoke a tactical language I had never heard from any other officer." He taught Marshall how to recognize the fundamental principles of war in action. "His problems were short and always contained a knockout if you failed to recognize the principle involved in meeting the situation. Simplicity and dispersion became fixed quantities in my mind, never to be forgotten. . . . He taught me all I have ever known of tactics." Marshall and his fellow students were proud to call themselves "Morrison men."[11] Labeled by some disparaging critics as the "Leavenworth clique," Marshall and others similarly trained prevented the inexperienced United States Army from being an embarrassment to the country in France during World War I.

Through extraordinary effort, Marshall finished at the top of the class in July 1907, thereby earning a place in the next year's Command and General Staff School, stepping-stone to the War College and thus to General Staff assignments. There he finished first again and was made an instructor at the school for the next two years. During the summers, the best Leavenworth students were assigned to instruct National Guard summer camps, a job most Regular Army officers regarded with distaste. But Marshall, a natural teacher, thrived in the outdoors instructing troops. The guardsmen were anxious to learn, he discovered, and he (now a first lieu-

11

tenant) could command units normally under majors or colonels. Marshall's empathy with the guard's problems, understanding of its limitations, ability to motivate its men, and belief in its crucial position as the foundation of America's ground forces clearly distinguished him from the sort of Regular the guard normally encountered.

Marshall's reputation as a premier staff officer attracted the attention of his peers and superiors, but twice—in August 1913, following maneuvers in Connecticut, and again in February 1914, when he successfully led the "invaders" in maneuvers in the Philippines—overwork brought him to the edge of a nervous breakdown. "I woke . . . to the fact that I was working myself to death, to my superior's advantage, and that I was acquiring the reputation of being merely a pick and shovel man. From that time on I made it a business to avoid, so far as possible, detail work, and to relax as completely as I could manage in a pleasurable fashion. Unfortunately, it was about six years before I could get away from details because they were in my lap."[12] Later, Marshall reiterated his lessons to other important subordinates who he feared were overworking, because their physical collapse would make them useless, both to their country and to him.[13]

Despite the costs to his health, Marshall's success in the 1914 maneuvers, during his second tour of the Philippines, was so noteworthy that Major General Hunter Liggett, and subsequently Major General J. Franklin Bell, had him made their aide-de-camp. As Bell's aide, he missed the opportunity to join John J. Pershing's punitive expedition into Mexico in 1916; instead, when he returned to the United States in July 1916, he became involved in the burgeoning preparedness movement, which was establishing officer training camps. Brigadier General William L. Sibert was impressed with Marshall's handling of a camp in California, and when Sibert was given command of the First Infantry Division in the spring of 1917, he asked Marshall to join his staff in the crucial role of assistant chief of staff for training and operations. Thus Marshall was the second man ashore in France when the first American troop ship docked at Saint-Nazaire on June 26, 1917.

The American Expeditionary Forces' first six months in France were crucial for Marshall's development as a leader. He also called it "the most depressing, gloomy period of the war," and he and his friends in the First Division referred to it as their "winter of Valley Forge."[14] Marshall saw firsthand the effects of American overconfidence, inexperience, and lack of preparation, particularly in contrast to the other combatants. Even with French assistance and limited combat, the initial United States divisions would not be ready for months, and Pershing and AEF General Headquarters were getting anxious to show that their decision to prepare an autonomous army was justified.

On October 3, 1917, Pershing and some of his staff arrived at First Division headquarters to witness a demonstration that Marshall (by this time a major) had had to arrange for them on short notice. After the exercise, Pershing was furious at what he considered an insufficiently cogent critique by General Sibert and his chief of staff. "He just gave everybody hell," Marshall recalled. "He was very severe with General Sibert . . . in front of all the officers . . . and generally he just scarified us. He didn't give General Sibert a chance to talk at all. . . . So I decided it was about time for me to make my sacrifice play. . . . I went up and started to talk to General Pershing. . . . He shrugged his shoulders and turned away from me, and I put my hand on his arm and practically forced him to talk." According to an officer who worked with him in 1918, when Marshall was angry, "his eyes flashed and he talked so rapidly and vehemently no one else could get in a word. He overwhelmed his opponent by a torrent of facts." "I was just mad all over," Marshall recalled; "I had a rather inspired moment."[15]

Afterward, General Sibert and the other staff officers thought that Marshall's actions had ruined him. But General Pershing was impressed; not only did he make a point on subsequent visits of seeing Marshall alone and seeking his opinions on the division's progress, but in mid-1918 he moved him to an important job at AEF General Headquarters and, in May 1919, made him an aide-de-camp. Over his career, Marshall would repeatedly demonstrate not only the vigor and eloquence with which he could defend crucial decisions that he was certain were correct, but also his failure to be intimidated by the mighty—as Franklin Roosevelt, Winston Churchill, Harry Truman, and others would later learn.

Marshall once permitted the pressure on him to push his anger beyond acceptable bounds. In December 1917, while acting chief of staff of the First Division (essentially second in command), his growing irritation with the staff at AEF General Headquarters for their "misun-

George C. Marshall as a first lieutenant, circa 1908. *The George C. Marshall Foundation*

derstanding of our situation" went too far. Nearly all of these men were friends and many also former students of his at Fort Leavenworth, "but we were wholly out of sympathy with each other, and I felt that they didn't understand what they were doing at all. They had become very severe and they didn't know what they were being severe about. . . . General Pershing was severe, so they modeled their attitude on him. I was so outraged by this that I talked a great deal and I made a great mistake." His attitude cost him the chance to become the division's permanent chief of staff, which would quickly have led to his promotion to brigadier general in 1918 instead of 1934.[16]

As head of First Division's operations section, Marshall prepared the report on the first American ground forces troops killed in combat, wrote the orders for the first American raid on German lines, and did much of the planning for the first American offensive at Cantigny. On June 18, 1918, Marshall formally asked for troop duty. First Division's commander, Major General

Robert L. Bullard, replied that he could not approve this request, "because I know that Lieut. Col. Marshall's special fitness is for staff work and because I doubt that in this, whether it be teaching or practice, he has an equal in the Army to-day."[17]

In mid-July 1918, Marshall was transferred to AEF General Headquarters at Chaumont, where he joined the First Army's operations section. He found the atmosphere there entirely different: the staff at Chaumont dealt with ocean tonnage, ports of debarkation, dock construction, tank manufacture, methods of training divisions, and the complexities of inter-Allied politics.[18]

In the year between Marshall's arrival in France and his transfer to the Chaumont headquarters, the AEF had grown in size and experience, and Pershing was preparing to launch it full-force against the now-weakening German army. Marshall's job was to prepare plans for the Saint-Mihiel salient offensive, scheduled for September 12, 1918, and for the far greater offensive on the Meuse-Argonne front, scheduled to begin on September 25. Marshall had to move 220,000 French and Italian soldiers out of one sector and move in some 600,000 U.S. and French troops, their supplies, and their equipment over the same constricted roads. His success added another Marshall legend to that of the brilliant young tactician of the Philippine maneuvers.[19]

The lessons learned by AEF officers during World War I strongly colored their thinking in the interwar period. Those officers landing in the summer and fall of 1918 saw a weakening German army and a burgeoning AEF, and thereafter they tended to overestimate the quality of American ground forces. But Marshall had suffered through AEF's painful and slow evolution toward military competence. Much of this pain occurred, he asserted, because Americans assumed that infantry training was simply a matter of taking up the trusty hunting rifle and marching off. Marshall thought that poorly written and taught school histories, awash with flag-waving but devoid of accurate military history, encouraged and sustained this dangerous myth.[20] Instead, as was demonstrated conclusively in France, army leaders had to provide American men with carefully crafted instruction and practice in order to fight modern wars.

Not only was extensive basic training needed for enlisted recruits, but equally important—perhaps more, considering the potential impact of faulty decision making—officers needed training in leading in the field; therefore, as the balance of power shifted against American interests between 1939 and 1941, Marshall insisted upon training in ever-larger maneuvers. Moreover, long service in the field under trying conditions demonstrated that officers—including colonels and generals—had to have physical stamina, or they would collapse under the strain, as many had done in France in 1918. Marshall's rule in World War II was that in order to receive a combat command, general officers, regardless of age, had to demonstrate that they had at least the physical stamina of a forty-five-year-old in good condition.[21]

Other lessons that Marshall derived from his experiences in France included a belief that officer candidates should not be taken merely from that then-narrow class of college students and graduates. He founded and stubbornly defended the Officer Candidate School system, even to the point of threatening to resign as army chief of staff in March 1941 if OCS was not implemented.[22]

Another lesson Marshall had learned in Lorraine's muddy fields was the importance to troop morale of medals and honors quickly awarded. He was much impressed when French Premier Georges Clemenceau appeared at the American front to hand out medals less than a day after the first AEF soldiers had been killed in November 1917. During World War II, Marshall pressed a reluctant President to acquiesce to various new awards for soldiers: the Good Conduct Medal, the Bronze Star, the infantryman's badges, and theater ribbons.

In May 1919, Marshall became one of General Pershing's three aides-de-camp, a position he held until departing for troop duty in China in mid-1924. These five years—spent helping Pershing wind up AEF affairs and then serving as Chief of Staff Pershing's office manager—constituted a postgraduate education in national and War Department politics for Marshall. Although they were not a new but a recurring pattern in American history, the post–World War I congressional hearings and investigations, the general lack of public interest in ground forces, and the consequent excessive defense budget cuts also taught Marshall important lessons about handling Congress and dealing with army public relations and the National Guard.

The concept of the small, professional army was entrenched in American tradition, and Marshall recog-

General John J. Pershing and Colonel George C. Marshall during their tour of French battlefields, August 1919. *The George C. Marshall Foundation*

nized that its role would be that of trainer and repository of administrative and technical expertise for the citizen-soldier army that would fight any future wars. The key question was thus what was the most effective form of reserve component. Marshall strongly and actively supported not only the National Guard but also the Reserve Officers' Training Corps and the Citizens' Military Training Camps movement. When the Civilian Conservation Corps was thrust upon the army in 1933, many professional officers viewed it as an unwelcome distraction. Marshall instead saw the opportunity for officers to acquire experience in working with masses of raw recruits.

In 1927, following the death of his wife, Marshall was given the opportunity to command the academic department of the Infantry School at Fort Benning, Georgia. Since 1919 the Regular Army had shrunk, promotion had stagnated, command opportunities had evaporated, and equipment grew scarcer and more obsolescent. Some professional officers slowly slipped into mental somnolence. Unfortunately, many officers who had seen the AEF at its peak in late 1918 believed that nothing needed to be changed. At the Infantry School, Marshall began his struggle against the intellectual coagulation of the "cast-iron Regulars."

Marshall made the Infantry School the fountainhead of army reform. Quietly and gradually, so as not to arouse opposition, Marshall brought into the faculty open-minded men recently returned from troop duty. "We bored from within without cessation during my five years at Benning," Marshall said after he left in 1932. He hammered incessantly on the theme of simplicity: no reading of long lectures containing only school-approved doctrine, no field exercises dependent upon possessing elaborate maps, no beautifully detailed orders from headquarters that stifled local initiative, no overblown intelligence estimates that harried commanders had no time to read, and no field procedures so complex that tired citizen-soldiers could not perform them. "Get down to the essentials," he directed. "Make clear the real difficulties, and expunge the bunk, complications and ponderosities." He was particularly aggrieved by "colorless pedantic form" used in army manuals, insisting upon clear, concise language, written to be absorbed by National Guard and Reserve officers, not just Regulars. Some two hundred future generals passed through the Infantry School as instructors or students during Marshall's tenure. And like Morrison before him, Marshall produced a group of ground forces officers who were proud to call themselves "Marshall's men."[23]

The Infantry School period was a happy one for Marshall, and in October 1930 he married Katherine Tupper Brown, a vivacious widow with three young children. In 1932, he was pleased to return to commanding troops, as he hated desk jobs and paperwork. But sixteen months later he was suddenly detailed to Chicago as senior instructor for the Illinois National Guard. He tried without success to get the assignment changed. The Thirty-third Division's commanding general had demanded that the War Department send him an outstanding professional officer, because civil unrest seemed likely in Chicago as the Great Depression staggered toward another bitter winter. Army Chief of Staff Douglas MacArthur wrote that Marshall "has no superior among Infantry Colonels."[24]

Given the numerous dangers to the professional officer's career that were inherent in service with the highly politicized National Guard, many officers took care to avoid risks.[25] Not Marshall. He undertook to reform guard training in Illinois and to reeducate the guard's officer corps, using his three years in Chicago as a proving ground for his citizen-soldier training ideas. Marshall also pressed the War Department to assign a higher caliber of Regular officers as guard instructors and to support them better. He worked hard at improving the Thirty-third Division's morale, stimulating increased interest in its activities and attacking the guard's relative isolation from the community it sought to serve. Marshall's successful efforts generated for him a company of staunch supporters in Illinois. This, along with his history of good relations with the reserve components, was extremely valuable during the 1940–1942 period when, as army chief of staff, he had to remove large numbers of ineffective guard officers, many of whom were replaced with Regulars. The political recriminations against the War Department were vigorous enough under Marshall; under anyone else they could have seriously disrupted the army's mobilization and modernization. Throughout World War II, Marshall insisted upon a sort of "affirmative action" policy regarding guard officer promotions. After the war, there was no recurrence of the anti-Regular Army backlash of 1919–1920 among the National Guard.

In October 1936, Marshall finally received his long-awaited general's star and was given command of the Fifth Brigade of the Third Division at Vancouver Barracks, Washington. He recalled this assignment with fondness for the rest of his life. At last he was back with troops, in a beautiful region of fish-filled rivers, and had a huge Civilian Conservation Corps district to oversee. This was Marshall's last restful assignment for many years. In July 1938 he was recalled to the War Department to head the War Plans Division. In October 1938 he became the army's deputy chief of staff, and by April 1939, President Roosevelt had decided to name him the next chief of staff.

On July 5, five days after Marshall became acting chief of staff, the President issued an executive order stating that the chief of staff and the chief of naval operations should report directly to himself on certain issues instead of through their civilian departmental heads. Marshall now had the access that was so desired in

Washington, but he knew that he would have to earn the President's confidence. Well aware of Roosevelt's affable and manipulative nature, Marshall insisted on keeping his own distance while maintaining his loyalty and his willingness to disagree with the President's ideas. He never visited the President in Hyde Park, New York, or Warm Springs, Georgia, despite his new friend (and Roosevelt confidante) Harry Hopkins's urgings. Marshall also asked the President to stop referring to the navy as "we" and the army as "they."[26]

George Marshall was sworn in as chief of staff of the United States Army on the morning of September 1, 1939, a few hours after the news had reached Washington of Germany's invasion of Poland. Prior to the attack on Pearl Harbor in December 1941, polls indicated that the public was pessimistic about the nation's ability to stay out of a Europe-wide conflict, but there was no desire to get involved; the only universally popular idea was the defense of the Western Hemisphere and American possessions. Both civilian and military personnel in the War Department reflected divided public opinion. While American military strategists generally agreed that Germany was the most dangerous of the Axis powers, their preparations for war were severely circumscribed. Significant progress in mobilizing American military and economic power began only with the shocking German victories in the spring of 1940.

President Roosevelt's gauging of the public's mood was generally accurate and his caution frequently justified, Marshall believed. The chief of staff was determined to operate as a member of a political-military team and not to adopt the traditional expedient of attempting to bypass the President's organizational and appropriations decisions via friends in Congress.[27] It was important for Marshall to demonstrate his nonpartisan role to both the executive and legislative branches. Marshall was successful in his efforts to insure cordial relations between the War Department and Congress; he was an effective witness, profoundly informed on military matters, better acquainted than most professional soldiers with the political difficulties besetting a legislator, and appreciative of the public's anxieties at the time. He appeared forty-eight times before various House and Senate committees between the summer of 1939 and the autumn of 1941.[28] An example of how many in Congress trusted Marshall more than "that

man in the White House" is reflected in a memorandum from Secretary of the Treasury Henry Morgenthau Jr. to President Roosevelt on May 15, 1940: "Let General Marshall, and only General Marshall, do all the testifying in connection with the Bill which you are about to send up for additional appropriations for the Army."[29]

The chief of staff's role between late 1939 and late 1941 was to modernize an army traumatized by penury and isolation for nearly a generation, a role for which Marshall was probably uniquely qualified. The United States Army (which included the Air Corps) counted but 165,000 officers and enlisted personnel as of July 1, 1939, and a year later it was only 50,000 larger. Germany's all-out attack on its western neighbors forced a radical change in Congress, leading to the passage of the first peacetime draft in United States history and the federalization of the National Guard. Suddenly, an ill-prepared Regular Army was inundated. Between the fall of France and the attack on Pearl Harbor, the army's air and ground forces increased 750 percent, threatening the whole antiquated system with overload and collapse. Meanwhile, equipment was still only trickling from the production lines, and a significant portion of that equipment had to be diverted to the Allies.

Marshall responded with enormous energy. Not only was he frequently before Congress; he was constantly on the move, visiting new cantonments, witnessing new weapons demonstrations, inspecting training facilities, observing maneuvers, and seeking effective leaders to promote. He frequently and unequivocally put officers on notice that he expected them to pay close attention to the quality of their troops' morale. Harried commanders could too easily delegate concern over command morale issues to junior officers or rely merely on paper directives to achieve results; Marshall's experience was that this was potentially disastrous. In mid-1941 he convinced Congress to grant him a contingency fund of $25 million to be used to circumvent the army's cumbersome financial procedures in morale-related expenditures.[30]

The lessons he had learned at AEF general headquarters and since made Marshall an advocate of interservice cooperation and unity of command. His interest in air power began when he was a student at Fort Leavenworth. He was constantly flying, and he required his staff officers and inspectors to fly. Marshall's belief in

General George C. Marshall and Secretary of War Henry L. Stimson witnessing the swearing-in of Oveta Culp Hobby as director of the Women's Army Auxiliary Corps by Major General Myron C. Cramer, judge advocate general, May 16, 1942, in Washington, D.C. *The George C. Marshall Foundation*

a balanced air-ground force, however, did not appeal to many strategic bombing enthusiasts, who were determined to create a separate air force. Marshall was certain that the pilot-dominated air service was far from ready to operate as an independent bureaucracy, so he made an informal agreement with his friend Air Forces Chief of Staff H. H. ("Hap") Arnold: Arnold would suppress the independence enthusiasts; Marshall would see to it that airmen gained the experience necessary to run a postwar independent organization. One of Marshall's most important moves was to elevate Arnold to membership on the Joint Chiefs of Staff when it was created in early 1942.[31] To keep the navy from feeling that Marshall might use his vote with that of his subordinate,

Arnold, to override naval ideas, Marshall suggested that Admiral William D. Leahy become chairman of the JCS.

Marshall's determination to achieve unity of command (i.e., all Allied military units in a particular theater under a single commander) resulted from his observation of disorganized Allied command on the western front in World War I prior to the appointment of Supreme Commander Ferdinand Foch in 1918. Three weeks after Pearl Harbor, Marshall convinced the reluctant British to create the American-British-Dutch-Australian Command in the Pacific, under Britain's Sir Archibald Wavell. This short-lived command established the precedent for a single Allied commander in such theaters as Europe (Dwight D. Eisenhower) and the

General George C. Marshall, standing fourth from left, posing for a photograph with members of the American and British chiefs of staff at Casablanca, January 1943. President Franklin D. Roosevelt and Prime Minister Winston Churchill are seated in front. *The George C. Marshall Foundation*

Mediterranean (Sir Harold Alexander). Indeed, one of Marshall's most constant and successful policies during World War II was strengthening the Anglo-American alliance, despite differing strategic interests.

The United States's first priority was to raise a large military force—although there was debate over its service distribution and ultimate size. Strategically, the United States was determined to concentrate on defeating Germany while holding the line against Japan, although after the Pearl Harbor attack, operations in the Pacific were far more aggressive than prewar plans had anticipated. To defeat Germany, the United States Army

desired to crack open *Festung Europa* and fight decisive artillery and mechanized battles in the relatively open and well-roaded country of northern France.

Marshall was reluctant to commit the United States to lengthy and expensive campaigns in the Mediterranean, as many British leaders preferred. While political necessity and military opportunism in 1942 and 1943 necessitated major Allied operational commitments to North Africa, Sicily, and Italy, Marshall rebelled at further investments in what he called the "suction pump" in the Mediterranean and forced a commitment to a spring 1944 invasion of Normandy:

Operation Overlord. As late as the Cairo Conference of December 1943, Marshall was the presumptive choice to be supreme allied commander for Europe, but given political and personality issues in other theaters that required Marshall's touch, the high regard in which he was held in the United States, and especially President Roosevelt's reluctance ("I feel I could not sleep at night with you out of the country"), Dwight D. Eisenhower was named to the post.[32]

Marshall was disappointed at losing this opportunity to lead the army he had created, but he accepted the decision—as was his duty and as he always did—without further comment. He was pleased with Eisenhower's performance. Marshall's philosophy was to pick good leaders (and he was rather proud of his success in this) and protect them from outside interference (especially from Washington), but relieve them quickly if they failed.

Given his confidence in his subordinates, Marshall's focus tended to be six months ahead of the current battle. For example, at the time of the Battle of the Bulge (December 1944–January 1945, which he regarded as a splendid opportunity for Eisenhower to deal harshly with the Germans), Marshall was concerned with occupation problems, Pacific strategy, and the coming massive movement of troops there, demobilization, and postwar military organization. American planning throughout the war had aimed at keeping its own casualties low, and raining mass destruction from the air had become commonplace. In consequence, Marshall had little difficulty accepting the use of atomic bombs on Japanese cities, particularly after the fierce Japanese resistance on Okinawa and Iwo Jima.[33]

Following V-J Day, Marshall was anxious to retire after nearly forty-four years of active duty, including six as army chief of staff, but the army had many demobilization problems to solve. Marshall was not permitted to retire until mid-November 1945. On November 27, less than twenty-four hours after his retirement ceremony, President Harry Truman called him back to duty for the thankless task of attempting to mediate between the Nationalists and Communists in China. Marshall's failure to achieve the impossible by arranging for Mao Tse-tung to acquiesce to Chiang Kai-shek's uncontested rule in China, and his subsequent opposition to significant American military involvement in the Chinese civil war, were major factors in causing him to be

General Marshall with American troops on an inspection tour in France following the Normandy invasion, June 1944. *The George C. Marshall Foundation*

branded, in the eyes of such conservatives as Senators William Jenner and Joseph McCarthy, as a Communist dupe or even an outright traitor.

In early 1946, President Truman asked Marshall to become secretary of state. Marshall's work in China delayed the appointment until January 1947. His tenure in the State Department was dominated by important international conferences; it lasted two years and coincided with a period of rapidly worsening Soviet-Western relations. The State Department had been a marginal player in foreign policy since 1933, and Marshall was appalled by its inefficient organization. Among his earliest acts were making Dean G. Acheson and then Robert A. Lovett his chief of staff (i.e., undersecretary of state), bringing in other men whom he knew to be superior organizers, operators, and intellects, and creating the Policy Planning Staff (reminiscent of the War Department's Operations Division), headed by Soviet scholar George F. Kennan.[34]

Of the dozens of noteworthy events and decisions that occurred during Marshall's tenure in the State

Secretary of State George C. Marshall participating in commencement exercises at Harvard University, June 5, 1947, where he is receiving an honorary law degree. In an address afterward, Marshall calls for a program of American aid for Europe, which becomes the Marshall Plan. *The George C. Marshall Foundation*

Department (for example, the Truman Doctrine, the Berlin Airlift, and the formation of NATO), the one that most Americans identify with him is the Marshall Plan—a title he himself never used, referring to it always as the European Recovery Program. The program was far more than a mere foreign-aid effort costing $13.3 billion and lasting four years; it included the reorganization of world trade and the modernization of European capitalism among its goals. Marshall's contribution, however, occurred during the crucial period of May 1947 to March 1948, when the idea and appropriation had to be sold to Congress and the American people.

By the spring of 1947 it had become clear to the Truman Administration's foreign policy leaders that Europe was facing a crisis. Business and trade were being disrupted by physical destruction, hunger, unemployment, social and financial turmoil, and declining civilian morale—particularly in Germany, Italy, and France; moreover, what remained of the war-inspired goodwill toward the Soviet Union had largely dissipat-ed, and many people feared the spread of Moscow-dominated Communism. During the unproductive Moscow Foreign Ministers' Conference in March and April, Ernest Bevin of Britain and Georges Bidault of France told Marshall of Europe's problems and dangers.

Marshall put his staff to work proposing solutions, and he decided to make an important speech at the Harvard University alumni convocation on June 5, 1947, following the commencement, where he received a long-delayed honorary degree. In a deliberately low-key ten-minute presentation, Marshall proposed that the European nations themselves take the initiative and prepare a cooperative program for presentation to the United States, that all European countries be invited to participate (although his advisers expected that the Soviet Union would decline), and that the American public understand the character of the problem and the remedies to be provided, for "the whole world's future" hung on this. Bevin and Bidault reacted swiftly to the challenge.

Marshall always believed that his contributions to the ERP were, first, insisting that the program originate in Europe and that it be open to all European states willing to abide by the rules, and second, campaigning successfully to line up support for the plan in the United States. Marshall's careful cultivation of Republican Senator Arthur Vandenberg, head of the Foreign Relations Committee, along with Congress's wartime admiration for Marshall and his nonpartisan stands put him in an excellent position to rally the pro-ERP troops against the widespread but relatively unorganized opposition to appropriating money for European recovery. "I worked on that as if I was running for the Senate or the presidency. That's what I am proud of," Marshall said later.[35]

Administration of the Marshall Plan (officially the Economic Cooperation Administration) was given to an independent agency, but Marshall had no antipathy to this. ECA Administrator Paul Hoffman later observed that he had "never known anyone who in my opinion was as completely selfless as General Marshall was in the handling of any problem"; he apparently never even considered how solutions would affect him or his public image and reputation in history.[36] In his memoirs, Georges Bidault, the French foreign minister, wrote that Marshall was "in a category all by himself . . . in uprightness and stature." Compared to Marshall, "the most bril-

The chief proponents for the Marshall Plan are pictured here, including President Harry S. Truman, Secretary of State George C. Marshall, Economic Cooperation Administration head Paul G. Hoffman, and the ECA's special representative to Europe, W. Averell Harriman. *UPI/Corbis—Bettmann*

liant reputations seem shabby. He was not vain; he spoke with great simplicity and humor about his career. . . . He was unaffected and did not pretend to be infallible. He would ask others for advice and could be unsure, even hesitant. But once he made up his mind, nothing could have made him change it. . . . He was quite cautious and sure enough of himself not to strike up rash poses or to speak off the cuff in public."[37]

Other than his role in the events leading up to the Pearl Harbor attack, few of Marshall's actions or decisions as chief of staff have evoked lasting public discussion, although historians continue to debate certain wartime decisions. His tenure as secretary of state was far more controversial, leading to such long-lasting disputes as his opposition to the recognition of a Jewish state in Palestine, his role in lowering the temperature of the Cold War, or his alleged failures regarding Nationalist China. But overall, historians have generally given him good marks for his handling of that difficult position in that trying time.

Marshall retired on the day of President Truman's second inaugural in January 1949. A kidney operation and its aftereffects kept Marshall out of public life until the summer of 1949, when he accepted the post of head of the American Red Cross, where his prestige and management expertise were needed to cure a number

Secretary of Defense George Marshall comments on Korean truce negotiations during a press conference at the Pentagon, July 1951. *The George C. Marshall Foundation*

of long-festering problems within the organization and to improve its public image, especially among veterans. He found himself traveling about the country again as he had during his efforts to sell the European Recovery Program. The outbreak of the Korean War in June 1950 only added to the burdens on the Red Cross and its leader.

The war brought to a head the increasingly hostile relations between President Truman and Secretary of Defense Louis Johnson, under whom Marshall had served between 1938 and 1940. The President once again asked Marshall to accept a difficult and largely thankless assignment, and Marshall replaced Johnson as secretary on September 21, 1950. The State Department was being run by Marshall's friend and former assistant, Dean Acheson; the chairman of the Joint Chiefs of Staff was Marshall protégé Omar Bradley; and Marshall was friendly with the three service chiefs. Consequently, during his year as secretary of defense, the potentially difficult problems of civilian-military and interservice relations were simplified and reasonably harmonious.

The epitome of the United Nations's success in the Korean War occurred at the Inchon landings, the week before Marshall became secretary of defense. His first important decision was to agree with the Joint Chiefs of Staff that Douglas MacArthur should be allowed to pursue the retreating North Koreans north of the Thirty-eighth Parallel, but within a few weeks he was trying to restrain MacArthur, lest he widen the war into Manchuria or provoke direct Soviet intervention. In the late winter and early spring of 1951, after the UN forces had recovered somewhat from their defeat by the Chinese, Marshall had to deal with MacArthur's increasingly public criticism of Truman administration policy in Korea and East Asia. He and the Joint Chiefs reluctantly agreed that MacArthur had too severely strained the subordination of the military to civilian rule, and they relieved him of command on April 10, 1951.

Marshall's support of MacArthur's relief provoked a storm of criticism, but this slowly blew over after the congressional hearings. The secretary of defense made an inspection trip to Korea, where the United Nations military force was under his protégé, Matthew Ridgway. As the end of his year in office approached, the battlefront in Korea was beginning to stabilize, and the diplomats were taking over the situation.

Marshall resigned on September 12, 1951, and was finally allowed to retire, except for his continuing participation in VMI affairs. On May 15, 1951, he was honored by his alma mater with the naming of one of the three arches in the cadet barracks after him (the others are named for George Washington and Stonewall Jackson). In December 1953 he received the Nobel Peace Prize for his role in the Marshall Plan.

George Marshall died, following a long illness, at Walter Reed Army Hospital on October 16, 1959, and was buried in Arlington National Cemetery. Winston Churchill wrote, not long before Marshall's death:

"In war he was as wise and understanding in counsel as he was resolute in action. In peace he was the architect who planned the restoration of our battered European economy. . . . He has always fought victoriously against defeatism, discouragement, and disillusion. Succeeding generations must not be allowed to forget his achievements and his example."[38]

Germany before the Marshall Plan—ruins engulf the Brandenburg Gate in Berlin at the end of the war, 1945. This monument, located in the Soviet zone of the city, became the symbol of a divided Germany when that country was partitioned in 1949.

The George C. Marshall Foundation

German men and women at work upon a block of apartments, funded in part by the Marshall Plan.

The George C. Marshall Foundation

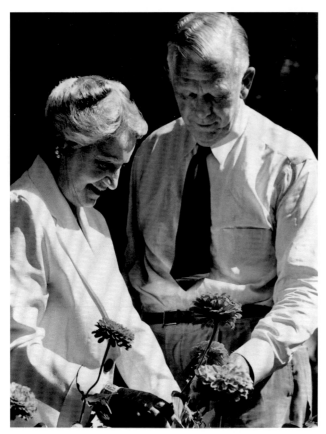

George C. Marshall at the time of his retirement, with his second wife, Katherine Tupper, relaxing outside of their home in Leesburg, Virginia, September 1951. *Time Inc.*

1. Larry I. Bland and Sharon Ritenour Stevens, eds., *The Papers of George Catlett Marshall* (Baltimore: Johns Hopkins University Press, 1981–), vol. 3, pp. 499, 501.

2. The definitive and authorized biography of General Marshall is Forrest C. Pogue's *George C. Marshall,* 4 vols. (New York: Viking Press, 1963–1987). Two valuable single-volume biographies are Mark A. Stoler, *George C. Marshall: Soldier-Statesman of the American Century* (Boston: Twayne Publishers, 1989), and Ed Cray, *General of the Army: George C. Marshall, Soldier and Statesman* (New York: W. W. Norton and Co., 1990).

3. Richard E. Neustadt and Ernest R. May, *Thinking in Time: The Uses of History for Decision-Makers* (New York: Free Press, 1986), pp. 247–48.

4. Larry I. Bland, ed., *George C. Marshall Interviews and Reminiscences for Forrest C. Pogue,* 3rd ed. (Lexington, Va.: George C. Marshall Foundation, 1996), p. 70 (hereafter cited as *Marshall Interviews*).

5. *Ibid.,* p. 99.

6. *Ibid.,* pp. 95, 97.

7. *Ibid.,* p. 119; Bland and Stevens, *Papers of George Catlett Marshall,* vol. 1, p. 11.

8. *Marshall Interviews*, p. 121.

9. *Ibid.,* pp. 142–43.

10. *Ibid.,* pp. 156–57.

11. Bland and Stevens, *Papers of George Catlett Marshall,* vol. 1, pp. 45–46.

12. *Ibid.,* vol. 2, p. 31. See also Pogue, *Marshall,* vol. 1, p. 124.

13. For example, see his efforts during the autumn of 1943 to convince Joseph Stilwell to take a vacation. *Ibid.,* vol. 4, pp. 135, 139, 220.

14. *Marshall Interviews,* p. 121.

15. *Ibid.,* pp. 197–98; Benjamin F. Caffey to Forrest C. Pogue, January 14, 1961, Research File, George C. Marshall Archives, Lexington, Virginia.

16. Bland and Stevens, *Papers of George Catlett Marshall,* vol. 1, p. 129.

17. *Ibid.,* vol. 1, p. 144.

18. *Ibid.,* vol. 1, p. 152.

19. Pogue, *Marshall,* vol. 1, pp. 174–79.

20. See his speeches on this in Bland and Stevens, *Papers of George Catlett Marshall,* vol. 1, pp. 219–22; vol. 2, pp. 123–27.

21. *Ibid.,* vol. 3, pp. 188, 464.

22. *Ibid.,* vol. 2, p. 512.

23. *Ibid.,* vol. 1, pp. 409–16; Pogue, *Marshall,* vol. 1, pp. 249, 269.

24. Bland and Stevens, *Papers of George Catlett Marshall,* vol. 1, p. 399.

25. *Ibid.,* vol. 1, p. 405.

26. *Ibid.,* vol. 2, p. 3; *Marshall Interviews,* pp. 610–11.

27. *Marshall Interviews,* p. 297.

28. On the importance of Marshall's testimony for mobilization, see Mark Skinner Watson, *Chief of Staff: Prewar Plans and Preparations,* a volume in *United States Army in World War II* (Washington, D.C.: Historical Division, Department of the Army, 1950), p. 8.

29. Bland and Stevens, *Papers of George Catlett Marshall,* vol. 2, p. 214.

30. *Ibid.,* vol. 2, pp. 505–7.

31. *Marshall Interviews*, pp. 310–15.

32. Bland and Stevens, *Papers of George Catlett Marshall,* vol. 4, p. 195.

33. On the decision to use atomic bombs, see *Marshall Interviews*, pp. 423–25.

34. Pogue, *Marshall,* vol. 4, pp. 146–50.

35. *Ibid.,* p. 244; *Marshall Interviews*, pp. 527, 556–57.

36. Pogue, *Marshall,* vol. 4, p. 256.

37. *Resistance: The Political Autobiography of Georges Bidault* (New York: Praeger, 1967), p. 114.

38. Churchill to John C. Hagen Jr., July 30, 1958, William J. Heffner Collection, George C. Marshall Archives.

A Personal Reflection on George C. Marshall

COLIN L. POWELL

George C. Marshall. The very mention of the name causes us to pause and reflect on this man and to reflect on his life. I don't think it is an exaggeration to say that George Marshall was one of the greatest Americans who has ever lived. Winston Churchill called him "the noblest Roman of them all" and "the last great American." Certainly to me he is in the top rank. I became more and more convinced of that fact the more senior I became, and especially as I grappled with the responsibilities of Chairman of the Joint Chiefs of Staff.

Throughout my military career, I turned to Marshall often for inspiration and wisdom. And the better I understood the challenges he had to face, the better I understood what a giant he truly was. What is it about George Marshall that stirs me? What is it about him that reaches across the years to touch so many Americans? He was certainly no flamboyant general, he was not a character, there were no pearl-handled revolvers or corncob pipes or crusty anecdotes to spice up the legend of Marshall. He never wrote a book to tell his story. He never ran for election to public office. He never sought popularity. He never exploited his fame. He never asked for recognition or favors. He was a man driven more than anything else by a sense of duty, by the powerful, overpowering obligation of service. To him it was never George C. Marshall who was important; it was the task at hand, it was the mission, it was the call

of his army, it was the call of his country. Service, service, always service. The quiet power of the man lay in his utter selflessness. It lay in the dignity that emerges from every photograph you've ever seen of him. It lay in his hard work and it lay in his immense personal sacrifice. It lay in his integrity, his compassion, his wisdom. George Marshall practically defined those virtues. Yet he would have thought it odd if you had tried to congratulate him for these things. To him, those virtues were simply expected of a citizen of this country. Duty was a value instilled in him as a cadet at the Virginia Military Institute, which he carried with him throughout his long public career, from the jungles of the Philippines in 1902 to Stockholm to receive the Nobel Peace Prize in 1953.

George Marshall helped to define the nation we have today. The die for him was cast in 1939, when he became the Chief of Staff of an army that was dismally unprepared for the coming war. It was Marshall, first and foremost, who fought to bring the army out of its prewar slumber. It was Marshall more than anyone else who brought together millions of GIs, the industrial power of the nation, and the strategic vision that went on to win World War II. It was Marshall about whom President Truman once said simply, but passionately, "He won the war." And it was the retired General of the Army Marshall, after forty-three years of service in uniform, after promising himself and his family a life of quiet privacy, who answered the phone on the very first day of his retirement in Leesburg. It was the President calling. The General was again needed. And so at the age of sixty-five, Marshall was propelled by the call of duty into what would be another six years of public service.

And in those years this quiet, dignified man of such monumental character succeeded in shaping the rest of the twentieth century. Without Marshall there might never have been the North American Treaty Organization, which helped win the Cold War. Without Marshall the policy of containment might only have been words. And without Marshall's leadership there might not have been a plan to rebuild Europe. In those three accomplishments alone, I doubt that there has ever been a more impressive record of success in the history of statesmanship.

Today, almost a half-century after his time in government, NATO is still a thriving alliance of democracies; it works. It works so well that it has already moved beyond the Cold War that inspired its birth and is adopting strategies and missions to meet the new challenges of a new era.

Marshall also threw his weight behind the idea of containment, an idea that was foreign to America's character but vital to her future—the notion that we should be strong even in peace, that we should use military might in peace to contain an enemy that threatened everything we held dear. Even now, with the Cold War over, military strength continues to be the cornerstone of our security and our best guarantee that another enemy will not emerge to challenge the world's new peace. But of course the Marshall Plan worked best of all, as the free and prosperous continent of Europe can testify. Without the Marshall Plan, I shudder to think of what might have happened to Europe. With a few simple words delivered in a modest speech at Harvard in June 1947, George Marshall set in motion the building of a new Europe based on democracy, self-determination, and mutual trust.

Excerpted from a speech given at the Marshall ROTC Awards Seminar at Virginia Military Institute, Lexington, Virginia, April 14, 1993

Catalogue

J A M E S G. B A R B E R

Marshall's felt campaign hat. *The George C. Marshall Foundation*

The Marshall children

LUCAS PHOTO GALLERY,
Uniontown, Pennsylvania

Platinum print, 14.6 x 10.2 cm.
(5 ¾ x 4 in.), 1884

The George C. Marshall Foundation

Born in Uniontown, Pennsylvania, on December 31, 1880, George C. Marshall Jr. (right) was four years old when this photograph was taken of him with his older siblings, Stuart and Marie. To Stuart, Marshall largely credited the awakening of his competitive spirit. Stuart had always been the superior student and had graduated from the Virginia Military Institute in good standing. When it came time for Marshall to think about going to college, he overheard Stuart plead with their mother not to allow him to attend VMI, lest he "disgrace the family name." Stuart's comment made an indelible impression upon Marshall. From that moment, he was determined to follow in his brother's footsteps, and as he described years later, to "wipe his face."

Marshall enters VMI

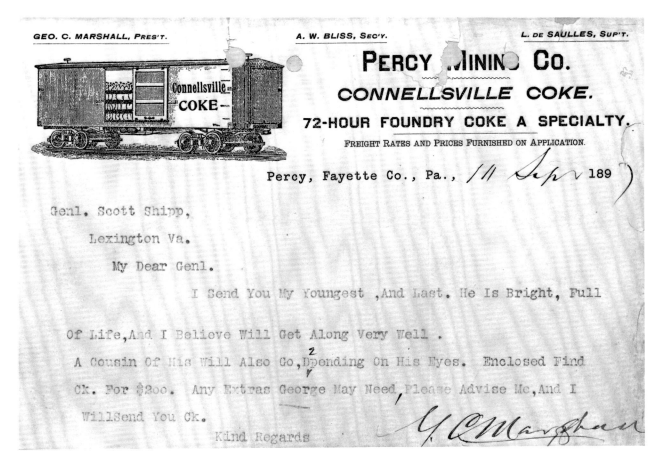

GEO. C. MARSHALL, PRES'T.   A. W. BLISS, SEC'Y.   L. DE SAULLES, SUP'T.

PERCY MINING Co.
CONNELLSVILLE COKE.
72-HOUR FOUNDRY COKE A SPECIALTY.
FREIGHT RATES AND PRICES FURNISHED ON APPLICATION.

Percy, Fayette Co., Pa., *11 Sep* 189

Genl. Scott Shipp,

    Lexington Va.

      My Dear Genl.

          I Send You My Youngest ,And Last. He Is Bright, Full

Of Life,And I Believe Will Get Along Very Well .

A Cousin Of His Will Also Go,Dpending On His Eyes. Enclosed Find

Ck. For $200. Any Extras George May Need,Please Advise Me,And I

WillSend You Ck.

        Kind Regards

George C. Marshall Sr.'s letter enrolling his son at the Virginia Military Institute, 1897

The George C. Marshall Foundation

George Marshall enrolled at the Virginia Military Institute in Lexington, Virginia, largely because of circumstances rather than heartfelt desire; he would have preferred to attend the United States Military Academy at West Point. But Marshall was only an average student, and he had suffered an injury to his right elbow that would have made passing West Point's physical examination difficult. In addition, obtaining the necessary political recommendation would have been awkward, because his father was a staunch Democrat in a Republican district. Therefore, in the fall of 1897, Marshall's father wrote to General Scott Shipp, superintendent of VMI: "I Send You My Youngest, And Last. He Is Bright, Full Of Life, And I Believe Will Get Along Very Well. . . . Enclosed Find Ck. For $200."

Unlike West Point, where the tuition was free, Marshall's attendance at VMI would exact personal sacrifices on the financially strapped family. Several years earlier, Marshall's father had lost heavily in a speculative land venture. Although the family was never destitute, Marshall learned early in life how to stretch a meager budget. This experience served him well at VMI and later in the army.

First Classman Marshall

MICHAEL MILEY AND SON,
Lexington, Virginia

Albumen silver print, 14 x 9.8 cm.
(5 ½ x 3 ⅞ in.), circa 1900

The George C. Marshall Foundation

"The V.M.I. in my day was a pretty stern affair," recalled George Marshall. "Life was exceedingly austere. There were no delicacies . . . no arrangements practically to amuse the cadets." At best, Marshall was never more than an average student. Yet the rigors of cadet life motivated him to excel. After his first year, Marshall held the highest positions of authority available. As his responsibilities increased, he strove to exercise them in ways that did not create resentment. In later years, as Marshall climbed the army's chain of command, he was widely respected for his forthright leadership.

Marshall was in his last year at VMI when this photograph was taken of him wearing his furlough uniform. He presented this picture to his sister Marie, and signed it on the back: "with much love—from your brother George."

Marshall-Coles wedding party

UNIDENTIFIED PHOTOGRAPHER

Left to right: Marie (Marshall's sister), Lily, George, Stuart, Mr. and Mrs. George C. Marshall Sr., and Mrs. Walter Coles (the bride's mother)

Gelatin silver print, 18.4 x 23.8 cm. (7 1/4 x 9 3/8 in.), 1902

The George C. Marshall Foundation

While a cadet at VMI, George Marshall met his future wife, Elizabeth ("Lily") Carter Coles (1874–1927). "She was a very lovely looking woman," said Marshall. "I guess you might call her a beauty." Lily lived with her mother in a house just off of the campus. She was "the finest amateur pianist" Marshall had ever heard, and her music and charm so captivated him that he routinely "ran the block" to see her. These visits were against school regulations and would be dismissal offenses if discovered. Because Marshall was the senior military officer of his class, he gambled that he was above suspicion. Moreover, he was in love.

The young couple were married on February 11, 1902, in a simple Episcopal ceremony inside the bride's home. The somber-looking wedding party pictured here on the Coles's front porch was not entirely a harbinger of things to come. The marriage was an extraordinarily happy one for twenty-five years, until Lily's death in 1927. She died of a heart condition that militated against a strenuous life or ever having children.

Colonel Marshall

Marshall as an aide-de-camp to General Pershing, Chaumont, France, 1919

UNIDENTIFIED PHOTOGRAPHER

Gelatin silver print, 21 x 15.9 cm.
(8 1/4 x 6 1/4 in.), 1919

The George C. Marshall Foundation

George C. Marshall began his forty-three-year career in the United States Army in 1902. Recognized by his superior officers for his efficient staff work, Marshall emerged from the battlefields of France in 1918 with his reputation enhanced. Work behind a desk was a dubious distinction for any ambitious young officer eager for the combat experience deemed essential for career advancement in the military. Yet at the end of World War I, Marshall, by this time a brevet colonel, accepted without protest Major General John J. Pershing's offer to be an aide-de-camp. He scarcely could have declined, even though this meant another five years behind a desk.

At the start, his new assignment involved ceremony. Marshall escorted Pershing, now an American icon, on victory parades and to state dinners in Europe and the United States. In 1921, Pershing became chief of staff, the army's highest peacetime position, and Marshall's desk duties increased appreciably. The rewards for Marshall were forthcoming, if not immediate. Foremost, Marshall secured a valuable mentor in Pershing, the most admired soldier of his era. Later, Pershing would recommend to President Franklin D. Roosevelt that Marshall be promoted to brigadier general, and he enthusiastically endorsed Marshall's own appointment as chief of staff in 1939.

General John J. Pershing

SIR WILLIAM ORPEN
(1878–1931)

Oil on canvas, 91.4 x 76.8 cm.
(36 x 30 ¼ in.), circa 1919

National Portrait Gallery, Smithsonian
Institution; gift of the International
Business Machines Corporation

An 1886 graduate of West Point and a veteran of the Spanish-American War, General John J. Pershing (1860–1948) commanded the American Expeditionary Forces in France during World War I. Stiff in bearing and stern in manner, Pershing was the consummate soldier and the ideal leader to represent the interests of the United States abroad. He insisted that American troops fight under their own colors, and prevented them from being routinely siphoned off to French and British units depleted by three years of trench warfare. Pershing also trained his army rigorously for open field maneuvers. In the fall of 1918, some 1,250,000 Americans participated in the Meuse-Argonne offensive, which helped weaken Germany's resolve to prolong the war. In preparation for that historic battle, Colonel George C. Marshall, assistant chief of staff with the First Army, was ordered to plan the transfer of 600,000 men and 2,700 guns over three roads in less than two weeks. It was a Herculean task, one that Marshall concluded "represented my best contribution to the war."

Afterward, as an aide-de-camp to Pershing, Marshall had a chance to observe the four-star general: "I have never seen anybody who could listen to as severe criticisms" of himself "just as though it was about a man in another county." Marshall's comment, in part, reflected their close working relationship. Following Pershing's retirement in 1924, Marshall made every effort to remember the General of the Armies: Marshall always sent his greetings on Pershing's birthday, and Pershing was the best man at Marshall's second wedding in 1930. Later, as chief of staff, Marshall regularly visited Pershing, by then an invalid at Walter Reed Army Hospital, to solicit his views on military affairs. Marshall even secretly revised plans for Pershing's military funeral, an event the strong-willed general delayed until 1948.

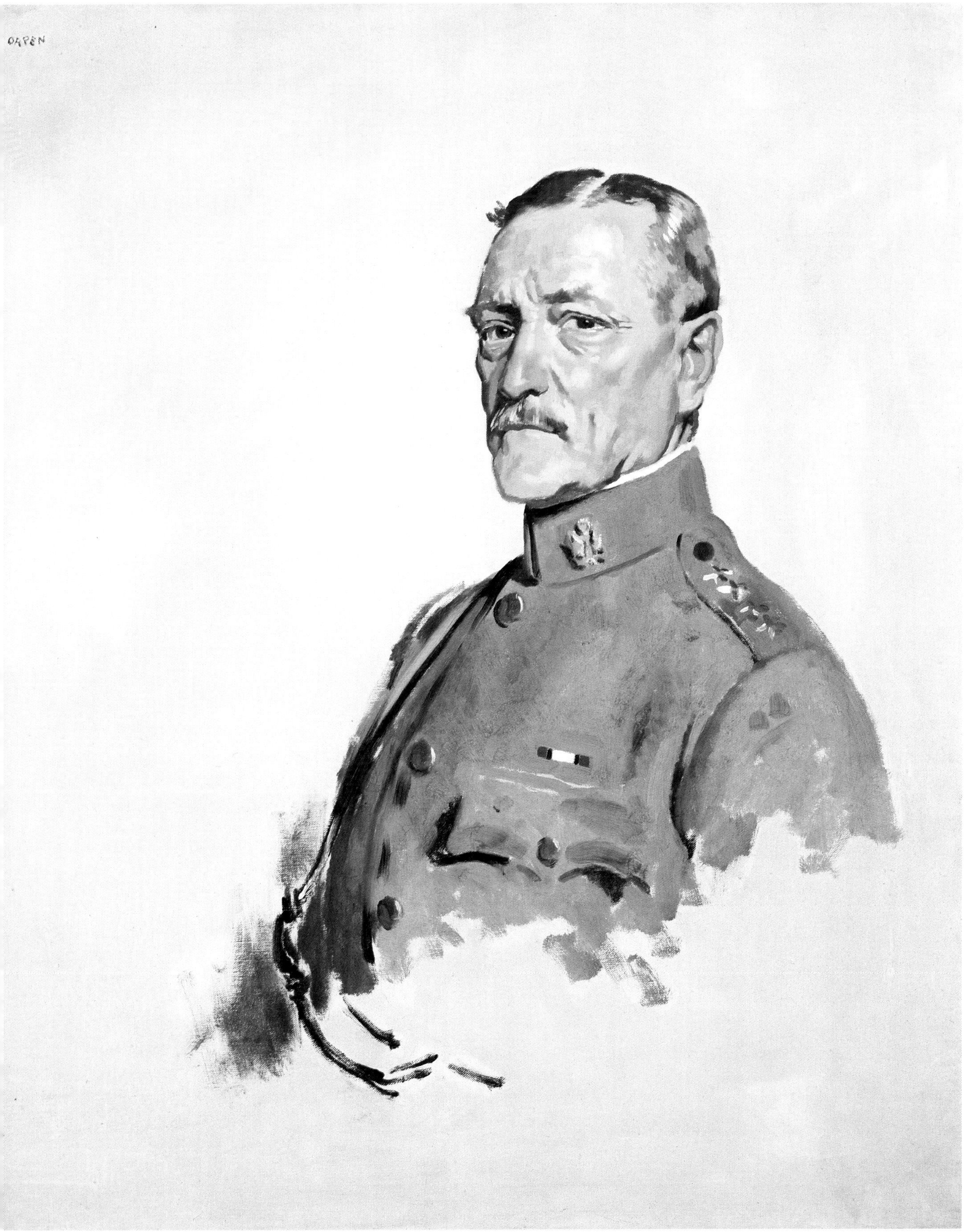
ORPEN

Marshall as chief of staff

ENIT KAUFMAN
(1897–1961)

Pencil on paper, 34.9 x 26.4 cm.
(13 ¾ x 10 ⅜ in.), 1942

Harry Ransom Humanities Research
Center, the University of Texas at Austin

On September 1, 1939, General George C. Marshall was sworn in as chief of staff of the United States Army. His rise to the army's highest peacetime position was ironic. Only the year before, he had complained to General Pershing: "I have so few years left for active service that I hate to lose them to desk instead of command work." Yet Marshall's entire career seemed to have been in preparation for this new assignment. By his own assessment, his chief qualifications for the job were that he had always "attended strictly to business and enlisted no influence of any sort at anytime." This was exactly the type of military adviser President Franklin D. Roosevelt desired in what promised to be perilous times ahead.

On Marshall's first day in office, Nazi Germany invaded Poland. With the start of World War II, the chief of staff's responsibilities grew immensely and soon became unprecedented when the nation declared war, following the Japanese attack on Pearl Harbor on December 7, 1941. Foremost, he had an army of fewer than 200,000 men to build into one of several million. He had to train that army with new techniques and equip it with new weapons. He had to muster national support for military preparations without inciting the wrath of isolationists. He had to revitalize the officer corps, an often-painful process of retiring his peers, many of whom he had known for years. He had to quell interservice rivalry, especially with the navy. He had to champion America's wartime interests against those of its allies, notably Great Britain. Ultimately, he had to win the confidence of President Roosevelt, who had selected Marshall largely on the recommendations of others. In time, Marshall proved to be indispensable, and was arguably the wisest appointment Roosevelt ever made as President.

General Marshall December 1947

Henry L. Stimson

ENIT KAUFMAN
(1897–1961)

Pencil on paper, 35.4 x 27.8 cm.
(13 ¹⁵⁄₁₆ x 10 ¹⁵⁄₁₆ in.), circa 1942

Harry Ransom Humanities Research
Center, the University of Texas at Austin

As civilian head of the army between 1940 and 1945, Secretary of War Henry L. Stimson (1867–1950) oversaw the largest expansion of the military in the nation's history. During Stimson's first year in office, the army grew more than fivefold and numbered more than a million and a half officers and men. The army would exceed eight million before World War II was over. Cumbersome war preparations might have taxed the energies of a much younger person, but Stimson, in his mid-seventies, proved to be remarkably resilient. As a former secretary of war (1911–1913), secretary of state (1929–1933), and governor general of the Philippines (1927–1929), he was a veteran statesman, thoroughly at home in the bureaucratic labyrinth of Washington. The common views he shared with Marshall had much to do with the unprecedented harmony enjoyed by civilian and military sectors in the War Department during a time of world crisis. The door was always open between these two chiefs, whose adjacent offices were models of integrity and decorum. They worked out their differences with the national interest in mind. The internment of Japanese Americans was a tragic exception. Stimson, a lawyer by training, ultimately accepted responsibility for this military decision about which he had had grave constitutional doubts. With Marshall, Stimson oversaw development of the atomic bomb. Yet as an admirer of Japanese history and art, he argued successfully against its use on the beautiful former capital, Kyoto, a shrine of Japanese culture.

"General . . .
You Didn't Know Nothin'!"

CLIFFORD K. BERRYMAN
(1869–1949)

India ink on paper, 34.3 x 36.2 cm.
(13 ½ x 14 ¼ in.), 1941

Prints and Photographs Division,
Library of Congress

For George Marshall, the critical moment of World War II occurred during the summer of 1941, five months before the United States entered the conflict. Congress was considering whether to extend the one-year-old Selective Service Act, which allowed the army to increase significantly by means of the draft. Marshall understood better than anyone the advantages to the enemy if the United States entered the war seriously outmanned, and he was determined not to let this happen. His dilemma, however, was to build a combat-ready army without provoking isolationists, who would be quick to blame the Roosevelt administration for pushing the nation into another foreign war.

This cartoon by Clifford K. Berryman appeared on the front page of the *Washington Star* on July 26, 1941, and depicted Congress's numerous concerns about the army in general and selective service in particular. As chief of staff, Marshall addressed these issues with a full and complete command of the facts before special congressional committees. He was unfailingly honest and above politics; in the end, he was rewarded by seeing the extension bill pass by one vote. The cartoonist underscored Marshall's political fight by alluding to General William T. Sherman's famous statement that "war . . . is all hell."

Franklin D. Roosevelt

George Marshall learned firsthand that engaging in a discussion with President Franklin D. Roosevelt (1882–1945) could at times be totally one-sided. If the President, famous for his congeniality and vacillation, preferred not to address an issue, he would unleash his charm and stage a monologue until the appointed hour was up. After one such performance, Marshall pleaded with the Commander in Chief for just three minutes in which to state his case for funding for military preparations. "I never haggled with the President," recalled Marshall. "I swallowed the little things so that I could go to bat on the big ones."

In time, Roosevelt valued Marshall's candor and relied upon his military judgments almost exclusively. At the start, however, their relationship was professionally stiff, in part because of Marshall's natural reserve. Marshall refused to be swayed by the President's charisma, to the point of not laughing at his jokes. Marshall's biographer has suggested that Roosevelt probably did not enjoy the general's company. For his part, Marshall deliberately avoided seeing Roosevelt, as a way of protecting his autonomy of command. Still, each man grew in the other's estimation. After Pearl Harbor, Marshall discovered that Roosevelt was indeed capable of swift and decisive action. And with each successful military operation launched from Marshall's desk, Roosevelt looked more and more to the chief of staff for ultimate victory. In naming Dwight D. Eisenhower supreme commander of the Allied Expeditionary Force, Roosevelt assuaged any disappointment Marshall may have felt at this missed opportunity with the comment, "I didn't feel that I could sleep at ease if you were out of Washington."

Winston Churchill

YOUSUF KARSH
(born 1908)

Gelatin silver print, 34.3 x 26.8 cm.
(13 ½ x 10 9⁄16 in.), 1941

National Portrait Gallery, Smithsonian
Institution

British Prime Minister Winston Churchill (1874–1965) was the most influential ally with whom the United States had to contend during the Second World War. In the opinion of President Roosevelt's trusted adviser Harry Hopkins, "*Churchill* is the gov't in every sense of the word—he controls the grand strategy and often the details. . . . The army, navy, air force are behind him to a man." Unfortunately for the Americans, Churchill had his own ideas about how to achieve victory in Europe. Whereas the American commanders argued for a massive invasion of France and Germany, Churchill was haunted by the hundreds of thousands of British casualties lost on the Continent during World War I. To avoid a similar bloody scenario, Churchill advocated a more peripheral strategy of attacking the Axis powers along the Mediterranean, particularly in North Africa, Italy, and the Balkans. In numerous strategy sessions, Marshall bristled at proposals that he considered to be "side shows," at times until the Prime Minister was "red hot." Marshall later felt that his own greatest contribution in the war was to keep Churchill in line with American battle strategy. In the end, as a measure of Marshall's success, Churchill called him "the true organizer of victory."

Yousuf Karsh of Ottawa took this photograph after Churchill had given a speech to the Canadian Parliament in late December 1941. (The text can be seen protruding from his pocket.) Karsh, a stickler for details, unintentionally induced a scowl after he plucked a new cigar out of Churchill's mouth just before clicking the shutter. Karsh remembered that "the silence was devastating," until Churchill smiled and allowed Karsh to take a second, friendlier picture.

This image of Churchill was widely published; it appeared in *Life* magazine in February 1942 and on the cover in May 1945. Karsh always believed it to be the picture that launched his long and successful career of photographing world celebrities. The cigar story became well known, and many of Karsh's future subjects would ask permission before smoking.

General Marshall

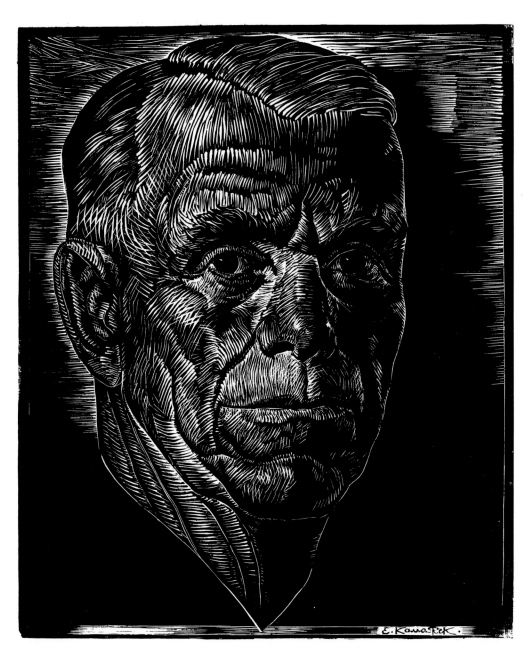

ELIAS KANAREK
(1901–1969)

Wood engraving, 24.3 x 19.8 cm.
(9 9/16 x 7 13/16 in.), circa 1950

National Portrait Gallery, Smithsonian
Institution; gift of the artist

Polish-born artist Elias Kanarek came to the United States in 1939 to paint the frescoes of the Polish Pavilion at the New York World's Fair. When the Nazis invaded Poland in September, Kanarek decided to remain in America. During the war years, he lived in Washington, D.C., where it is believed he made this wood engraving of Marshall.

Honoring the casualties of war

General Marshall presenting the Distinguished Service Medal to the widow of Colonel Carl D. Silverthorne, August 1944

The George C. Marshall Foundation

General Marshall extends his deep sympathy in your bereavement. Your husband fought valiantly in a supreme hour of his country's need. His memory will live in the grateful heart of our nation

The deaths of American servicemen overseas affected millions of relatives and friends back home. George Marshall was no exception; his stepson was killed in Italy in May 1944. Throughout the war, Marshall reported the Army's casualties every few days to President Roosevelt to apprise him of the nation's great human toll.

In this photograph General Marshall presents the Distinguished Service Medal to Alice Carey Silverthorne. Her husband, Colonel Carl D. Silverthorne, was overseeing operations for the chief of staff in Saipan in June 1944, when he was killed by an enemy sniper's bullet. Their daughter, Alice, observes the simple but memorable ceremony inside the newly completed Pentagon building.

The chief of staff's engraved sympathy card

The George C. Marshall Foundation

With the rise in American casualties, Marshall could no longer send bereaved parents and wives personal letters of sympathy. Instead, his office began mailing engraved condolence cards. Most households were grateful to receive them. Yet the card embittered some recipients; the mother of an infantryman killed in action recommended that Marshall "save the Government's funds."

Dwight D. Eisenhower

HARRY WARNECKE
(1900–1984)

Color carbro print, 40.6 x 32.5 cm.
(16 x 12 ¹³⁄₁₆ in.), 1945

National Portrait Gallery, Smithsonian
Institution; gift of Elsie M. Warnecke

General Dwight D. Eisenhower (1890–1969) was the closest any soldier ever came to being George Marshall's protégé. Eisenhower joined the General Staff in December 1941, and proceeded to excel at every leadership test to which the chief of staff could subject him. "George Marshall was rather a remote and austere person," recalled Ike, going by the nickname everyone in the army had used since he entered West Point. Marshall, however, always addressed him by his last name, and Eisenhower quickly discovered that Marshall's reputation for being all business was true in every respect. Eisenhower impressed his chief with his "brains, imagination and diplomacy." Still, there was in Eisenhower the unassuming Kansas schoolboy; one colleague considered Ike's disarming grin to be "worth an army corps in any campaign."

Marshall especially valued Eisenhower's natural ability to get along with people. This was a major consideration in 1942, when he sought an American commander capable of melding with the British high command overseas. Eisenhower demonstrated his combat prowess by leading the Allies to their first victory in North Africa. When asked by the President who should become supreme commander in 1943, Marshall in effect deferred to Eisenhower by refusing to put his own name forward. Eisenhower became the war's most visible general, the one who methodically organized the D-Day invasion of France, and who ultimately spearheaded the Allied victory over Germany. Eisenhower deserved his laurels, and Marshall was the first to congratulate him. Yet both men fully understood who had laid the cornerstone for his achievements.

General Marshall

HARRY WARNECKE
(1900–1984)

Color carbro print, 40.8 x 32.9 cm.
(16 1/16 x 12 15/16 in.), 1944

National Portrait Gallery, Smithsonian
Institution

This photograph of General Marshall was taken by Harry Warnecke, a pioneer of color photography. Warnecke was a staff photographer for the *New York Daily News*. The paper published a special Sunday picture section in which it began introducing color images. Warnecke suggested using color portraits on the covers and built a special color-separation camera to produce them. At the time of Marshall's sitting, in 1944, Warnecke's studio at the *Daily News* was attracting celebrities of every description—soldiers, statesmen, and movie stars alike.

John G. Dill and George Marshall

Dill and Marshall visiting the Custis-Lee Mansion, Arlington, Virginia, April 1942

The George C. Marshall Foundation

Throughout most of the war, Field Marshal Sir John G. Dill (1881–1944) headed the British Joint Staff mission in Washington. His official duties as a liaison were to smooth relations between the British and American allies. For Marshall, however, Dill proved to be considerably more than a mere go-between. A close relationship developed between these two soldiers, one that Marshall benefited from immensely. This was due in part to President Roosevelt's peculiar tendency to communicate with the British on military matters without notifying his own War Department. In a strictly confidential arrangement—one that would have placed Dill in great jeopardy had it ever been discovered—Dill agreed to share with Marshall all pertinent military correspondence between Roosevelt and Churchill. "It was a rather curious set up," Marshall remembered, "but a very effectual one." Because of Dill, Marshall was better able to coordinate military operations between the two allies. At one point, fearing that Churchill had become suspicious of Dill's American ties and might recall him, Marshall arranged for Dill to receive an honorary degree from Yale. As a final expression of his gratitude, Marshall won congressional approval to have Dill's body interred in Arlington National Cemetery when Dill died in 1944.

General Marshall

NISON A. TREGOR
(born 1904)

Bronze, 53.3 cm. (21 in.) height, 1943

The George C. Marshall Foundation

This bust of George Marshall was executed from life by Nison A. Tregor, about the time the artist was serving in the United States Army as a first lieutenant. Tregor plied his craft principally in military circles. Other works by him include busts of Douglas MacArthur, Dwight D. Eisenhower, and Omar N. Bradley. The bust of Marshall was presented by E. A. Tracey to the Virginia Military Institute in 1943.

General Marshall

AL HIRSCHFELD
(born 1903)

Watercolor, gouache, ink, and graphite on board, 42 x 28.5 cm. (16 ½ x 11 ¼ in.), 1945

National Portrait Gallery, Smithsonian Institution

George Marshall appeared on the covers of dozens of news magazines and popular journals. He was infrequently caricatured, however. This exception by Al Hirschfeld was the original drawing for the cover of the *American Mercury* in June 1945.

Hirschfeld, primarily a caricaturist of theater personalities, took pride in his economy of line, in evidence here. He considered his most successful likenesses to be those in which the subject began to assume the look of the drawing. By that standard, his caricature of Marshall never approached his best work.

General Marshall

JAMES ANTHONY WILLS

(born 1912)

Oil on canvas, 107.9 x 79.1 cm.
(42 1/2 x 31 1/8 in.), 1949

National Portrait Gallery, Smithsonian
Institution; transfer from the National
Museum of American Art; gift of the
International Business Machines
Corporation to the Smithsonian
Institution, 1962
[Not in exhibition]

James Anthony Wills painted several portraits of George Marshall in the late 1940s. He executed this three-quarter-length canvas from life sittings inside the Marshall residence, Dodona Manor, in Leesburg, Virginia. The Marshalls favored the artist's work and had a copy made for their home, as well as a portrait of Katherine Tupper Marshall (1882–1978), the general's second wife. The original, illustrated here, was in the collection of the International Business Machines Corporation until 1962, when it was presented to the Smithsonian Institution. Wills painted a portrait of Marshall in civilian dress for the State Department (illustrated on page 75), and his likeness of Dwight D. Eisenhower is the official White House portrait of the thirty-fourth President.

"The High Command"

Left panel: General Dwight D. Eisenhower, Secretary of War
Henry L. Stimson, General Douglas MacArthur

Right panel: Admiral Chester W. Nimitz, Secretary of the Navy
James V. Forrestal

AUGUSTUS VINCENT TACK
(1870–1949)

Oil on canvas, central panel, 242.6 x 246.4
cm. (95 ½ x 97 in.); side panels, 243.8 x
182.9 cm. (96 x 72 in.) each, 1947–1949

National Portrait Gallery, Smithsonian
Institution; partial gift of the Phillips
Collection

At the time of his death in July 1949, Augustus Vincent Tack had been working for several years upon a large triptych of President Truman and his military advisers at the end of World War II. Tack, an experienced mural and abstract painter, was encouraged by his patron, Duncan Phillips, founder of the Phillips Collection in Washington, and by David E. Finley, director of the National Gallery of Art. It was their hope that Congress would purchase these paintings for the future National Portrait Gallery. Tack had sittings with most of the subjects, including President Truman and General George Marshall, the two most central figures. Tack, however, died before completing this grand work. Phillips acquired the three canvases and his estate donated the largely finished central panel to the new National Portrait Gallery in 1968. The Gallery has subsequently acquired the two smaller side panels.

Central panel: Admiral William D. Leahy, General Henry H. Arnold, President Truman, General Marshall, Admiral Ernest J. King

Harry S. Truman

GEORGE TAMES
(1919–1994)

Gelatin silver print, 31.8 x 23.9 cm.
(12 ½ x 9 7/16 in.), circa 1949

National Portrait Gallery, Smithsonian
Institution; gift of Frances O. Tames

As private individuals, President Harry S. Truman (1884–1972) and General George C. Marshall had little in common. Truman was talkative, sociable, and enjoyed spending evenings around a card table, drinking bourbon with friends. Marshall, on the other hand, avoided social gatherings and never seemed comfortable letting down his reserve. After dining at the Marshall home in Leesburg, Virginia, Truman marveled at how Marshall's own family called him "colonel." Yet as public officials, Truman and Marshall shared traits that won each other's admiration. Chief among them, both leaders were forthright in making decisions of national importance. Neither man, for instance, ever had doubts about the decision to use atomic weapons against Japan.

Moreover, both men shared the same philosophy of public service. "The objective is the thing," wrote Truman, "not personal aggrandizement." Marshall could not have stated it better, nor was there anyone else in government who better exemplified this creed than George Marshall. Truman therefore dealt Marshall the public-duty card time and again, which the conscientious general could never decline. Only days after Marshall retired as chief of staff in November 1945, Truman sent him to China to mediate a peace between the Chinese Nationalists and the insurgent Chinese Communists. Unsuccessful, Marshall returned home a year later to become secretary of state. And at the age of sixty-eight, Marshall served as secretary of defense.

For Truman, Marshall was a "tower of strength and common sense." He also lent the administration a measure of prestige, especially with congressional Republicans. When an aide suggested that the multibillion dollar plan to revive Europe be named after the President, Truman explained that Congress would never accept anything less than the "Marshall Plan."

"Some China to Mend"

EDWIN MARCUS
(1885–1961)

India ink on paper, 29.8 x 29.8 cm.
(11 ¾ x 11 ¾ in.), 1945

Prints and Photographs Division, Library
of Congress

China was one of the world's unsolvable problems during the post–World War II era. This country of four hundred million inhabitants was enmeshed in a protracted civil war between the Nationalist government under Chiang Kai-shek and the Communists of Mao Tse-tung. The Japanese occupation of North China and Manchuria between 1936 and 1945 had temporarily cooled the internal conflict, while the two factions directed their belligerence toward a common enemy. But with the Japanese surrender, China again turned upon itself. Although the United States officially recognized Chiang's Nationalists, it supported a coalition government if that would bring peace. Toward that end, President Harry Truman sent George Marshall as a special envoy to China in 1945.

In this cartoon, which appeared in the December 2 issue of the *New York Times*, Edwin Marcus portrayed Marshall's task of rebuilding peace in China. The success of his mission was doubtful from the start, and a year of intense negotiations only convinced him of the futility of the situation. "Fear, distrust and suspicion between the rival parties," reported Marshall, "has been the greatest obstacle to the realization of peace and unity in China." His mission an acknowledged failure, Marshall returned home in January 1947 to undertake broader international duties as secretary of state.

Chiang Kai-shek and Madame Chiang Kai-shek

CARL M. MYDANS
(born 1907)

Gelatin silver print, 34 x 27 cm.
(13 ⅜ x 10 ⅝ in.), 1941

Prints and Photographs Division, Library of Congress

As the leader of the Republic of China, Generalissimo Chiang Kai-shek (1887–1975) professed to have had a vision of transforming his country into a modern industrial power. Throughout the 1940s, the United States supported this goal with generous financial aid and military expertise, in the hope that China would become a great and stable force in Asia. Reality, however, proved to be bitterly different from the dream. Much of the disappointment had to do with Mao Tse-tung's rival Communist Party, which was intent upon taking over the country. A great deal of Chiang's energies and resources were directed toward fending off this growing Communist threat. But Chiang himself was an obstacle to his country's economic and social progress, at least as far as American envoys in China were concerned. Their consensus was that Chiang, as an administrator and military leader, was indifferent to the internal corruption that was crippling his government. "If Chiang had cared about or even had directed his attention to the woeful plight of the Chinese people," concluded Marshall, "he could have knocked the props out from under Mao."

Madame Chiang Kai-shek (born 1898?), shown with her husband in this photograph for *Life* magazine by Carl Mydans, was unofficially her country's most influential ambassador. Educated in the United States, she was well-spoken, beautiful, and charming; and on numerous occasions she served as her husband's interpreter. Diplomats, including George Marshall, regarded her as Chiang's best asset. Her friendship with Marshall was genuine, and was perhaps the only endearing thing he took home with him from China.

64

Man of the Year

ERNEST HAMLIN BAKER
(1889–1975)

Watercolor on board, 27.3 x 23.5 cm.
(10 ¾ x 9 ¼ in.), 1947

The George C. Marshall Foundation

In January 1947, any disillusionment George Marshall brought back with him from his failed China mission quickly dissipated in his new role as secretary of state. After reorganizing the department, which had been largely inefficient and underutilized since the days of the Roosevelt administration, Marshall concentrated his energies on maintaining peace in Europe. The intransigence of the Soviet Union, intent upon sowing Communism in the postwar depression, proved to be his and the free world's greatest obstacle. Four hundred million dollars in aid for Greece and Turkey, and a speech by the President, which became the Truman Doctrine, committed the United States to the defense of democracy abroad. In June, Marshall gave new impetus to the concept of American largesse in an address following commencement at Harvard University. The ideas he put forth would inspire what became known as the Marshall Plan, a multibillion dollar incentive for free countries in Europe to rebuild their economies and infrastructures.

"As the man who offered hope to those who desperately needed it," George Marshall was *Time* magazine's Man of the Year for 1947. This portrait by Ernest Hamlin Baker was the original cover art for that issue. Between 1940 and 1947, Marshall appeared on the cover of *Time* a total of six occasions, more than anyone else during this period, including Roosevelt, Truman, MacArthur, Eisenhower, and Churchill. Marshall had also been Man of the Year in 1943.

Joseph Stalin

SAMUEL J. WOOLF
(1880–1948)

Oil on canvas, 60.9 x 50.8 cm. (24 x 20 in.),
1937

National Portrait Gallery, Smithsonian
Institution; gift of Muriel Woolf Hobson

At five feet, five inches in height, Joseph Stalin (1879–1953) was the small, unassuming-looking dictator of the Soviet Union. Yet he was the absolute ruler of some 180 million people whose empire spanned across Europe and Asia from Poland to the Pacific Ocean. After suffering humiliating defeats by Hitler on the Russian front in 1941–1942, Stalin's Red Army systematically vanquished the Nazis in Eastern Europe as far west as Berlin. At the Potsdam Conference in July 1945, when an American mentioned this achievement, Stalin replied matter-of-factly that Czar Alexander had gotten to Paris. Inevitably, Stalin's allies were left to decipher his postwar intentions. Soviet expansionism lurked behind them all and was the political motive that prevented the Russians from engaging in meaningful peace agreements. In Moscow in 1947, Secretary of State George Marshall found Stalin to be "completely evasive" about substantive issues, while maintaining a calm and gracious exterior. "Stalin's greatness as a dissimulator was an integral part of his greatness as a statesman," wrote Russian expert George Kennan. "An unforewarned visitor would never have guessed what depths of calculation, ambition, love of power, jealousy, cruelty, and sly vindictiveness lurked behind this unpretentious facade."

This portrait by Samuel J. Woolf appeared on the cover of *Time* magazine on December 20, 1937.

68

"This One Talks!"

JOHN CHURCHILL CHASE
(1905–1986)

India ink with tonal film overlay on paper,
39.3 x 30 cm. (15 ½ x 11 ¹³⁄₁₆ in.), 1954

Prints and Photographs Division, Library
of Congress

This caricature of Soviet Foreign Minister Vyacheslav Molotov (1890–1986) is reminiscent of the man himself, whose participation at peace conferences in Paris (1946), Moscow, and London (1947) was tantamount to a monkey wrench in the peace process, especially in the talks concerning the future of Germany and the autonomy of Eastern Europe. As a diplomat, Molotov was stubborn and dogged; the Americans nicknamed him "Iron Pants" for his ability to log long hours at the bargaining table. In the press, he became symbolic of Russian obstructionism: His favorite tactics included bickering over rules and procedures and needlessly reiterating Soviet viewpoints. Too often on matters of real substance put forth by his counterparts from the United States, Great Britain, and France, Molotov's customary response was "No!" On a personal level, Secretary of State George Marshall found Russia's highest ranking deputy to be agreeable and informative, especially about his early association with Stalin and the Bolshevik Revolution of 1917. "But his attitude completely changed," recalled Marshall, "the minute it was business."

John Chase's caricature *This One Talks!* appeared in the *New Orleans States* on February 7, 1954. In trying to evoke a more forceful image, Molotov had, at the age of sixteen, adopted his last name from the Russian word *molot*, meaning hammer.

George F. Kennan

NED SEIDLER
(lifedates unknown)

Oil and gouache on board, 25.4 x 26.7 cm.
(10 x 10 ½ in.), 1947

National Portrait Gallery, Smithsonian
Institution; gift of Time, Inc.

As chargé d'affaires in Moscow in the mid-1940s, George F. Kennan (born 1904) understood the Russian Marxist way of thinking better than any other American. Nevertheless, Kennan was little appreciated outside of diplomatic circles in Washington, and within those circles his early warnings about Soviet behavior largely went unheeded. Then in 1946 he had the occasion to send an extraordinarily long telegram (8,000 words) back to Washington, underscoring the centuries-old "Russian sense of insecurity" and opportunism that welded the Kremlin "fanatically to the belief that with the U.S. there can be no permanent *modus vivendi*." Subsequent diplomatic failures with Moscow to reach peace accords for Germany and Austria gave credence to Kennan's views. He warned that freedom in Europe would be dangerously compromised unless the United States forged strong Western alliances. In the spring of 1947, Kennan was tapped to head the State Department's newly established Policy Planning Staff, a select group of intellectuals whom Secretary George Marshall had organized to advise on matters of foreign policy. Under Kennan's direction, the Planning Staff devised the basic principles of the Marshall Plan.

Next to his long telegram, Kennan's most influential writing was his "X-Article," published anonymously in the July 1947 issue of *Foreign Affairs*, in which he advanced the theory of "containment" in dealing with the Russians. Although he offered no specifics about how the United States might check the Soviets square-for-square, containment became the policy of the Truman administration. But when the emphasis shifted from peaceful negotiating strategies to more military ones based upon atomic weapons, Kennan dissented. His influence ebbed, and he resigned from the State Department in 1950. Recalling Kennan's significance, former Secretary of State Henry Kissinger wrote, "Kennan came as close to authoring the diplomatic doctrine of his era as any diplomat in our history."

Ned Seidler's portrait of Kennan was an unused cover for *Time*'s July 28, 1947, issue. The image was taken from a photograph by Alfred Eisenstaedt.

Secretary of State Marshall

JAMES ANTHONY WILLS
(born 1912)

Oil on canvas, 74.9 x 62.2 cm.
(29 ½ x 24 ½ in.), 1949

Diplomatic Reception Rooms,
U.S. Department of State

Notwithstanding George Marshall's long and distinguished military career, students of history will always associate him foremost as the author of the European Recovery Program, more commonly known as the Marshall Plan. The idea of extending billions of American dollars for foreign economic recovery was not Marshall's alone, however. He was only one among many Western leaders who foresaw the tragic consequences of doing nothing for those countries in which basic living conditions were deplorable and still deteriorating, two years after the end of World War II. Winston Churchill likened Europe to "a rubble heap, a charnel house, a breeding ground of pestilence and hate." Food, fuel, shelter, and raw materials all were in desperate supply. In Germany, cigarettes were commonly used in place of money. Ideological conflicts only contributed to the prevailing mood of despair. A failure to reach peace agreements with the Soviet Union over Germany's postwar destiny prompted Marshall's poignant analogy, "The patient is sinking while the doctors deliberate."

In an address at Harvard University on June 5, 1947, Secretary of State George Marshall articulated the general principles of the Marshall Plan, based on the recommendations of his Policy Planning Staff. In gist, Marshall was offering to help Europe help itself: "Our policy is directed not against any country or doctrine but against hunger, poverty, desperation and chaos. Its purpose should be the revival of a working economy in the world so as to permit the emergence of political and social conditions in which free institutions can exist."

The Marshall Plan was generally acclaimed as a success in its day and has admirably withstood the rigors of historical inquiry. It has set the standard by which foreign aid projects have been judged ever since. Between 1948 and 1951, sixteen participating nations received more than thirteen billion dollars with which to improve agricultural and industrial production and to rebuild housing, medical, and transportation facilities. Although the Marshall Plan did not fully restore and integrate the economies of Western Europe, it nevertheless went far toward eradicating conditions of despair. On a human level, it gave new hope to hundreds of thousands.

Arthur H. Vandenberg

GEORGE TAMES
(1919–1994)

Gelatin silver print, 34 x 26.5 cm.
(13 3/8 x 10 7/16 in.), 1948

National Portrait Gallery, Smithsonian
Institution; gift of Frances O. Tames

Senator Arthur H. Vandenberg (1884–1951) of Michigan was pivotal in winning congressional support for the Marshall Plan. He chaired the Senate Foreign Relations Committee and was the Republican Party's spokesman for foreign policy. As one observer noted, he "was in the very heart of the inner circle that ran the Senate." In matters where he presided, nothing was ever accomplished without his consent and input. Consequently, he was the legislator with whom George Marshall worked closest in writing the resolution for the Marshall Plan. Vandenberg, a big, balding man with a rosy complexion and a penchant for cigars, liked being involved in groundbreaking legislation. Before the war, he had been a staunch isolationist. Afterward, he was a vanguard of the nation's bipartisan foreign policy. His enthusiasm for aid to Europe clearly demonstrated the extent of his conversion. "On his own typewriter," recalled Marshall, Vandenberg helped transform a vague concept into a "practical proposition." Without "his leadership and coordination in the Senate, the plan would not have succeeded." With a nod to Vandenberg's pride, the Truman administration endorsed his selection of Paul G. Hoffman—president of the Studebaker motor corporation and a fellow Republican—to head the Economic Cooperation Administration, which would administer the plan.

Dean Acheson

GARDNER COX
(1906–1988)

Oil on canvas, 88.9 x 63.5 cm.
(35 x 25 in.), 1974

National Portrait Gallery, Smithsonian
Institution; gift of Covington and Burling

Dean Acheson (1893–1971) was the consummate statesman of his time; he looked and played the role to perfection. The upright son of the Episcopal bishop of Connecticut, he had the eastern establishment credentials one might expect of a Harvard-trained lawyer-turned-diplomat. His air was stiffly formal, his suits were meticulously tailored, and his mustache smacked of British high society. Acheson conveyed a self-confidence, wrote one acquaintance, as big as any in the city of Washington, the capital of big egos. Indicative of this, Acheson titled his memoirs *Present at the Creation*. Intelligence and vision, however, were the qualities that defined Acheson's statesmanship; as secretary of state between 1949 and 1953, he was a principal architect of America's foreign policy at the start of the Cold War.

Acheson was George Marshall's chief deputy in foreign affairs in 1946 and 1947. From his State Department office, he facilitated Marshall's negotiations in China. When Marshall became secretary, Acheson, as under secretary, administered the department and implemented its reorganization. A month before Marshall made his historic speech at Harvard, Acheson gave a preliminary aid-to-Europe address at a state teachers' college in Mississippi. Lacking his boss's reputation and stature, Acheson was largely ignored or criticized; Senator Arthur Vandenberg objected to his commitment of taxpayers' dollars without congressional approval.

This portrait is a replica made by the artist after a life sitting in 1950. Acheson's former law firm, Covington and Burling, donated it to the National Portrait Gallery in 1974.

Marshall defends his plan

GEORGE TAMES
(1919–1994)

Gelatin silver print, 34.1 x 26.5 cm.
(13 7/16 x 10 7/16 in.), 1947

National Portrait Gallery, Smithsonian
Institution; gift of Frances O. Tames

The Marshall Plan galvanized Western Europe with new hope; the British foreign minister exulted: "I grabbed it with both hands." Yet the idea, reported *Time* magazine, "flew in the face of all the vows that Republican Congressmen made—and the public at election time had approved—to cut taxes, end Government controls, end Government spending. It was a promissory note for billions of U.S. dollars." Selling the plan to the American people proved to be a formidable task for the Truman administration. Marshall personally flew thousands of miles throughout the country, extolling the virtues of helping Europe to farmers, industrialists, businessmen, and women's organizations. "Putting the damned thing over" was what gave Marshall the greatest pride. Marshall was superb in his testimony before Congress, reported James Reston of the *New York Times*: "He was clear. He was calm. He was patient and courteous. And yet he acted like a man who was determined to get substantially the Marshall Plan he wanted or, as is already rumored in the capital, retire at last to Leesburg."

The politics of recovery

Posters designed for an international competition sponsored by the European Recovery Program, 1950

The German Marshall Fund of the United States

Austria

From the Stalinist point of view, the Marshall Plan seemed suspiciously like American interference in the internal affairs of Europe. The Russians refused to participate and forced those Eastern European countries under their influence—Czechoslovakia, Poland, Yugoslavia, Romania, Bulgaria, Hungary, Finland, and Albania—to decline as well. The Soviets countered with the Molotov Plan, named for Russia's foreign minister, which amounted to brokered trade agreements with their satellites. The fallacy was that the Russians had little to exchange in the way of machines and manufactured goods, the things Eastern Europe needed most for long-term reconstruction.

These European Recovery Program posters represent the spirit of unity and cooperation that the Marshall Plan fostered in the sixteen countries that accepted American assistance.

France

Netherlands

"Intra-European Co-operation for a Better Standard of Living" was the theme of an international poster contest sponsored by the ERP in 1950, as part of its public relations campaign. More than ten thousand entries were submitted in local competitions. The posters shown here were among twenty-five award-winning designs selected by a panel of graphic art specialists, each representing a Marshall Plan country. Reyn Dirksen of the Netherlands won the first prize with a nautical design titled *All Our Colours to the Mast*.

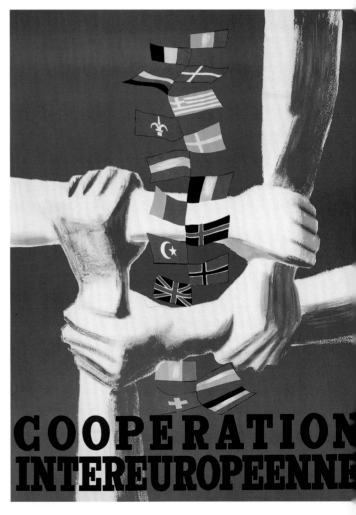

France

United Kingdom

Austria

85

George C. Marshall

THOMAS EDGAR STEPHENS

(1886–1966)

Oil on canvas, 127 x 101.6 cm.
(50 x 40 in.), circa 1949

National Portrait Gallery, Smithsonian
Institution; transfer from the National
Gallery of Art; gift of Ailsa Mellon
Bruce, 1951

In spite of his international stature, Marshall was portrayed in paintings and sculpture surprisingly few times. Marshall was himself largely responsible for this dearth. Always a man of limited patience, he allowed himself few interruptions. This was particularly true in the 1940s, when his official duties assumed worldwide status. Too often, his modesty and full schedule discouraged portrait sittings. The forty-five-minute session he gave to photographer Yousuf Karsh in 1944 was something of an exception. Karsh recalled that throughout the sitting, Marshall was "flatteringly agreeable and helpful." Several years later, British-born portraitist Thomas Edgar Stephens encountered a different Marshall altogether. While sitting for the oil portrait shown here, Marshall, then secretary of state, suddenly got up and left the room, and did not return. Later an aide explained to the bewildered artist that Marshall had thought of something urgent he needed to do. Stephens, however, succeeded in painting a lifelike portrait, one that Marshall highly approved.

Douglas MacArthur

HOWARD CHANDLER CHRISTY
(1873–1952)

Oil on canvas, 139.7 x 101.6 cm.
(55 x 40 in.), 1952

National Portrait Gallery,
Smithsonian Institution; gift of
Henry Ostrow

In September 1950, as George Marshall was beginning his new—and last—public duties as secretary of defense, his contemporary, General Douglas MacArthur (1880–1964), was successfully driving North Korea's Communist army back across the border, the Thirty-eighth Parallel. In command of United Nations forces in South Korea, MacArthur was capping an illustrious military career that spanned almost half a century. A West Point graduate, MacArthur was the most decorated veteran of World War I; at age fifty he had become the youngest chief of staff in the history of the United States Army. At Marshall's urging, MacArthur was presented with the Medal of Honor (the only major award he had not received) for service in the Pacific theater during World War II. On board the battleship *Missouri*, MacArthur presided over the Japanese surrender before going to Japan to oversee that nation's historic enactment of a constitutional government that renounced war. His persona in newsreels and on magazine covers was like that of an "aging movie idol," who looked much younger than his seventy years.

Notwithstanding his accomplishments and immense popularity in the United States, MacArthur had been at odds with American foreign policy since before the start of World War II, when he was the commander in the Philippines. Specifically, he believed that America's frontiers were in Asia and that Communism should be stopped in that hemisphere at all costs. When his views became public in the spring of 1951, contrary to the administration's decision not to escalate the war in Korea north of the Thirty-eighth Parallel, President Truman was forced to relieve MacArthur of his command once and for all. As secretary of defense, Marshall accepted the decision, but cautioned the President about the inevitable political fallout. Within weeks, Marshall was to feel the repercussions in a slanderous attack from Wisconsin Senator Joseph McCarthy. Although McCarthy's allegations of duplicity were superfluous, they were bristling to Marshall on the eve of his final retirement from public service.

"Oh, Brother!"

REGINALD MANNING
(born 1905)

India ink with opaque white on paper,
36.8 x 27.9 cm. (14 1/2 x 11 in.), 1951

Prints and Photographs Division, Library
of Congress

This cartoon by Reg Manning for the May 21, 1951, issue of the *Arizona Republic* criticized the Truman administration, specifically Secretary of Defense George Marshall and Secretary of State Dean Acheson, for fighting a limited war in Korea. It typified the view of conservative Republicans, who accused Truman of being soft on Communism and denounced his decision to relieve General MacArthur of command.

Manning, a popular syndicated cartoonist, won the 1951 Pulitzer Prize for another graphic commentary on the Korean War.

Joseph R. McCarthy

Ernest Hamlin Baker
(1889–1975)

Gouache on board, 22.9 x 20.6 cm.
(9 x 8 1/8 in.), 1951

National Portrait Gallery, Smithsonian
Institution; gift of Ernest and Louise
Frankel

Elected to the Senate in 1946, Joseph McCarthy (1908–1957) of Wisconsin went to Washington with a burning desire "to do something." During the war, he had served in the Pacific as an intelligence officer with the Marine Corps. McCarthy later embellished his service record with boasts of having been a tail gunner; the press reported that he allegedly "used to shoot up everything in sight, on the theory that any coconut tree might hide" the enemy. Once in the Senate, McCarthy used much this same rationale in his crusade against supposed Communists in government. In 1950, he accused the State Department of harboring 205 "Reds." Yet when pressed for names of suspected individuals, he could not produce a single traitor. The recent fall of China to Communism only encouraged McCarthy to "keep boring in" to find scapegoats. Harry Truman's Democratic administration provided the Republican McCarthy with several targets—in addition to the President and Secretary of State Dean Acheson, there was George C. Marshall. In 1946, Marshall had been Truman's personal envoy to China. McCarthy blamed his failure to bring peace to that divided nation on incompetence and on the administration's lack of will to stem Communism in Asia. In 1950, he charged Marshall with being "completely unfit" for the cabinet post of secretary of defense. After Truman fired General MacArthur the following year, McCarthy attacked Marshall again for his acquiescence. In a nearly three-hour-long speech on the floor of the Senate, McCarthy accused Marshall of making "common cause with Stalin." All but three senators walked out on him. "If I have to explain at this point," Marshall told the press, "that I am not a traitor to the United States, I hardly think it's worth it." Undaunted by the general's popularity, McCarthy published his speech, ghostwritten by a zealous Washington journalist, under the title *America's Retreat from Victory: The Story of George Catlett Marshall*.

McCarthy's portrait by Ernest Hamlin Baker appeared on the cover of *Time* on October 22, 1951, about when his book was published.

The Nobel Peace Prize

Marshall receiving the Nobel Peace Prize, 1953

The George C. Marshall Foundation

George Marshall was finally able to retire to the peace and solitude of his estate in Leesburg, Virginia, in the late summer of 1951. He had tried to leave the hectic duties of government service at the end of World War II, but fate intervened. The European Recovery Program, enacted when Marshall was sixty-seven, was to be his most enduring legacy. For his selfless efforts to foster peace in the postwar era, Marshall was awarded the Nobel Peace Prize in 1953. This was the first time the honor had ever been bestowed upon a professional soldier. Marshall is pictured in this photograph receiving the prize from Nobel Prize Committee President Gunnar Jahn at Oslo University in Norway, on December 10, 1953.

Nobel Peace Prize

Gold, 6.4 cm. (2 ½ in.) diameter, 1953

The George C. Marshall Foundation

94

Eulogy to Marshall

BILL MAULDIN
(born 1921)

India ink and charcoal with opaque white
on paper, 44.8 x 33.3 cm. (17 5/8 x 13 1/8 in.),
1959

The George C. Marshall Foundation

Marshall's health deteriorated progressively in the last years of
his life. The victim of a stroke, he spent his final days in
Walter Reed Army Hospital. He died on October 16, 1959.
Following his wishes, his funeral service at Arlington National
Cemetery was simple and unpretentious, and did not include a eulogy.

Bill Mauldin, through his famous World War II characters, Willie and
Joe, observed the somber event in this untitled cartoon for the *St. Louis
Post-Dispatch*.

Notes on Sources

Page 28: "Disgrace the family name," in Larry I. Bland *et al.*, eds., *George C. Marshall Interviews and Reminiscences for Forrest C. Pogue* (Lexington, Va.: George C. Marshall Foundation, 1991), p. 40 (hereafter cited as *Marshall Interviews*). "Wipe his face," *ibid.*

Page 30: "The V.M.I. in my day," *Marshall Interviews*, p. 115. "Life was exceedingly austere," *ibid.*, p. 116.

Page 31: "She was a very lovely looking woman," *Marshall Interviews*, p. 94. "The finest amateur pianist," *ibid.*

Page 34: "Represented my best contribution to the war," in Larry I. Bland and Sharon R. Ritenour, eds., *The Papers of George Catlett Marshall*, vol. 1 (Baltimore: Johns Hopkins University Press, 1981), p. 160. "I have never seen anybody," *Marshall Interviews*, p. 111.

Page 36: "I have so few years left," *Marshall Papers*, vol. 1, p. 598. "Attended strictly to business," *ibid.*, p. 642.

Page 42: "I never haggled with the President," in Forrest C. Pogue, *George C. Marshall* (New York: Viking Press, 1963–1987), vol. 2, p. 23. "I didn't feel that I could sleep," *Marshall Interviews*, p. 344.

Page 44: "*Churchill* is the gov't," in David Fromkin, *In the Time of the Americans* (New York: Alfred A. Knopf, 1995), p. 418. "The true organizer of victory," in Pogue, *Marshall*, vol. 3, p. xi. "The silence was devastating," Yousuf Karsh, *In Search of Greatness: Reflections of Yousuf Karsh* (New York: Alfred A. Knopf, 1962), p. 67.

Page 46: "It was a rather curious set up," *Marshall Interviews*, p. 414.

Page 47: "Save the Government's funds," Pogue, *Marshall*, vol. 3, p. 102.

Page 48: "George Marshall was rather a remote and austere person," Dwight D. Eisenhower, *At Ease: Stories I Tell to Friends* (Garden City, N.Y.: Doubleday, 1967), p. 248. "Brains, imagination and diplomacy," *Time* 45 (January 1945): 22. "Worth an army corps," in Eric Larrabee, *Commander in Chief: Franklin Delano Roosevelt, His Lieutenants and Their War* (New York: Harper & Row, 1987), p. 412.

Page 60: "The objective is the thing," Robert H. Ferrell, ed., *Off the Record: The Private Papers of Harry S. Truman* (New York: Harper & Row, 1980), p. 134. "Tower of strength," *ibid.* "Fear, distrust and suspicion," Ed Cray, *General of the Army: George C. Marshall, Soldier and Statesman* (New York: W. W. Norton, 1990), p. 564.

Page 64: "If Chiang had cared," in Cray, *General of the Army*, p. 573.

Page 66: "As the man who offered hope," *Time* 51 (January 1948): 18.

Page 68: "Completely evasive," *Marshall Interviews*, p. 342. "Stalin's greatness as a dissimulator," George F. Kennan, *Memoirs, 1925–1950* (Boston: Little, Brown, 1967), p. 279. "An unforewarned visitor," *ibid.*

Page 70: "But his attitude completely changed," *Marshall Interviews*, p. 343.

Page 72: "Russian sense of insecurity," in Gregg Herken, "The Great Foreign Policy Fight," *American Heritage* 37 (April 1986): 70. "Kennan came as close," in Walter Isaacson and Evan Thomas, *The Wise Men: Six Friends and the World They Made* (New York: Simon and Schuster, 1986), p. 24.

Page 74: "A rubble heap," in William Manchester, *The Glory and the Dream* (Boston: Little, Brown, 1973), p. 434. "The patient is sinking," in Pogue, *Marshall*, vol. 4, p. 200. "Our policy is directed," in James P. Warburg, *Put Yourself in Marshall's Place* (New York: Simon and Schuster, 1948), p. 26.

Page 76: "Was in the very heart," Dean Acheson, "Journey into Our Times," *American Heritage* 11 (February 1960): 79. "On his own typewriter," in Harry B. Price, *The Marshall Plan and Its Meaning* (Ithaca, N.Y.: Cornell University Press, 1955), p. 65. "His leadership and coordination in the Senate," *ibid*.

Page 80: "I grabbed it with both hands," *Time* 51 (January 1948): 19. "Flew in the face of all the vows," *ibid*. "Putting the damned thing over," *Marshall Interviews*, p. 527. "He was clear," in Cray, *General of the Army*, pp. 621–22.

Page 84: "Flatteringly agreeable and helpful," Yousuf Karsh, *Faces of Destiny: Portraits by Karsh* (Chicago and New York: Ziff-Davis, 1946), p. 100.

Page 86: "Aging movie idol," *Time* 53 (May 1949): 32.

Page 90: "To do something," *Time* 58 (October 1951): 21. "Used to shoot up everything," *ibid*., p. 23. "To keep boring in," *ibid*., p. 21. "Completely unfit," in Thomas C. Reeves, *The Life and Times of Joe McCarthy* (New York: Stein and Day, 1982), p. 278. "Common cause with Stalin," in *Time* 58 (October 1951): 24. "If I have to explain," in Cray, *General of the Army*, p. 723.

For Further Reading

Bland, Larry I., *et al.*, eds. *George C. Marshall Interviews and Reminiscences for Forrest C. Pogue.* 2nd ed. Lexington, Va.: George C. Marshall Research Foundation, 1991.

Cray, Ed. *General of the Army: George C. Marshall, Soldier and Statesman.* New York: W. W. Norton, 1990.

Isaacson, Walter, and Evan Thomas. *The Wise Men: Six Friends and the World They Made*. New York: Simon and Schuster, 1986.

Larrabee, Eric. *Commander in Chief: Franklin Delano Roosevelt, His Lieutenants, and Their War.* New York: Harper & Row, 1987.

Marshall, Katherine Tupper. *Together: Annals of an Army Wife*. New York: Tupper and Love, Inc., 1946.

Pogue, Forrest C. *George C. Marshall*. 4 vols. New York: Viking Press, 1963–1987.

Price, Harry B. *The Marshall Plan and Its Meaning*. Ithaca, N.Y.: Cornell University Press, 1955.

Stoler, Mark A. *George C. Marshall: Soldier-Statesman of the American Century*. Boston: Twayne Publishers, 1989.

Wilson, Rose Page. *General Marshall Remembered*. Englewood Cliffs, N.J.: Prentice-Hall, Inc., 1968.

Index

PHOTOGRAPHY CREDITS

National Park Service: p. 46

United States Army Signal Corps: pp. 18, 19, 20, 47

Rolland White and Marianne Bell Gurley: pp. 2, 35, 43, 45, 49, 51, 52,
55, 57, 58, 59, 61, 69, 73, 77, 79, 81, 82, 83, 84, 85, 87, 89, 93

Wide World Photos: pp. 11, 21, 95

Edited by Frances Stevenson and Dru Dowdy

Designed by Gerard A. Valerio, Bookmark Studio

Composed in Centaur and Bembo
by Sherri Armstrong, Typeline

Printed by Schneidereith & Sons, Baltimore